SPECTRUM®

Test Prep

Grade 2

Published by Spectrum®
an imprint of Carson-Dellosa Publishing LLC
Greensboro, NC

Visit *carsondellosa.com* for correlations to Common Core State, national, and Canadian provincial standards.

Spectrum®
An imprint of Carson-Dellosa Publishing LLC
P.O. Box 35665
Greensboro, NC 27425 USA

Table of Contents

What's Inside?

This workbook is designed to help you and your second grader understand what he or she will be expected to know on standardized tests.

Practice Pages

The workbook is divided into two sections: English Language Arts and Mathematics. The practice activities in this workbook provide students with practice in each of these areas. Each section has practice activities that have questions similar to those that will appear on the standardized tests. Students should use a pencil to fill in the correct answers and to complete any writing on these activities. If needed, passages may be read aloud to the student.

National Standards

Before each practice section is a list of the national standards covered by that section. These standards list the knowledge and skills that students are expected to master at each grade level. The shaded *What it means* sections will help to explain any information in the standards that might be unfamiliar.

Mini-Tests and Final Tests

When your student finishes the practice pages for specific standards, your student can move on to a mini-test that covers the material presented on those practice activities. After an entire set of standards and accompanying practice pages are completed, your student should take the final tests, which incorporate materials from all the practice pages in that section.

Final Test Answer Sheet

The final tests have a separate answer sheet that mimics the style of the answer sheets the students will use on the standardized tests. The answer sheets appear at the end of each final test.

How Am I Doing?

The *How Am I Doing?* pages are designed to help students identify areas where they are proficient and areas where they still need more practice. They will pinpoint areas where more work is needed as well as areas where your student excels. Students can keep track of each of their mini-test scores on these pages.

Answer Key

Answers to all the practice pages, mini-tests, and final tests are listed by page number and appear at the end of the book.

To find a complete listing of the national standards in each subject area, you can access the following Web sites:

The National Council of Teachers of English: www.ncte.org
National Council of Teachers of Mathematics: www.nctm.org/standards

English Language Arts Standards

Standard 1 *(See pages 7–12.)*
Students read a wide range of print and nonprint texts to build an understanding of texts, of themselves, and of the cultures of the United States and the world; to acquire new information; to respond to the needs and demands of society and the workplace; and for personal fulfillment. Among these texts are fiction and nonfiction, classic and contemporary works.

Standard 2 *(See pages 13–15.)*
Students read a wide range of literature from many periods in many genres to build an understanding of the many dimensions (e.g., philosophical, ethical, aesthetic) of human experience.

What it means:
- **Genre** is the type or category of literature. Some examples of genre include fiction, biographies, poetry, and fables. Each genre is characterized by various differences in form. For example, the fable differs from the broader category of fiction because it has a moral or character lesson.

Standard 3 *(See pages 16–21.)*
Students apply a wide range of strategies to comprehend, interpret, evaluate, and appreciate texts. They draw on their prior experience, their interactions with other readers and writers, their knowledge of word meaning and of other texts, their word identification strategies, and their understanding of textual features (e.g., sound-letter correspondence, sentence structure, context, graphics).

What it means:
- Students should use different strategies while they are reading to comprehend and make connections. Some of these strategies may include recognizing story characteristics; distinguishing fact from opinion; making inferences; determining the meaning of unknown words based on context; and interpreting information from pictures, diagrams, charts, or graphic organizers.

Standard 4 *(See pages 24–28.)*
Students adjust their use of spoken, written, and visual language (e.g., conventions, style, vocabulary) to communicate effectively with a variety of audiences and for different purposes.

Standard 5 *(See pages 29–33.)*
Students employ a wide range of strategies as they write and use different writing process elements appropriately to communicate with different audiences for a variety of purposes.

Standard 6 *(See pages 34–38.)*
Students apply knowledge of language structure, language conventions (e.g., spelling and punctuation), media techniques, figurative language, and genre to create, critique, and discuss print and nonprint texts.

Standard 7 *(See page 41.)*
Students conduct research on issues and interests by generating ideas and questions, and by posing problems. They gather, evaluate, and synthesize data from a variety of sources (e.g., print and nonprint texts, artifacts, people) to communicate their discoveries in ways that suit their purpose and audience.

English Language Arts Standards

Standard 8 *(See pages 42–43.)*
Students use a variety of technological and informational resources (e.g., libraries, databases, computer networks, video) to gather and synthesize information and to create and communicate knowledge.

Standard 9 *(See page 45.)*
Students develop an understanding of and respect for diversity in language use, patterns, and dialects across cultures, ethnic groups, geographic regions, and social roles.

What it means:
- A **dialect** is a regional variation in vocabulary, grammar, and pronunciation within a single language used by members of a group. It is a manner of expression that can lead to comprehension difficulties, if the dialect is particularly strong. Social roles and ethnic groups can be identified by use of specific dialects. Teaching a respect for diversity in language use and patterns can help build a global society.

Standard 10
Students whose first language is not English make use of their first language to develop competency in the English language arts and to develop understanding of content across the curriculum.

Standard 11 *(See page 46.)*
Students participate as knowledgeable, reflective, creative, and critical members of a variety of literacy communities.

Standard 12 *(See page 47.)*
Students use spoken, written, and visual language to accomplish their own purposes (e.g., for learning, enjoyment, persuasion, and the exchange of information).

Name _____ Date _____

1.0

Understanding Fiction

Reading and Comprehension

DIRECTIONS: Read the paragraph below. It tells about a girl who thinks it would be great if no one could see her. Then, answer the questions.

Example:

Read the story below and answer the question that follows.

   Camels are strong, sturdy animals that live in the desert. Camels are able to live in the desert because their bodies are designed for it.

What is the main idea?

(A) camels

(B) the desert

(C) bodies

(D) sturdy animals

Answer: (A)

If Cassie Were Invisible

   Cassie kicked at the dirty clothes on her floor. She was upset. Her dad told her to clean her room. Cassie wished she were invisible. Then, she wouldn't have to clean anything! If she were invisible, she would go to school and not do any work. She would stay up late. She would never have to take baths. Best of all, her brother couldn't pick on her. But, wait! If she were invisible, she wouldn't get any apple pie. No one would ask her to play. Cassie would never get to hug her grandparents. Maybe being invisible wouldn't be so much fun after all.

---

1. **In the beginning, why does Cassie want to be invisible?**

(A) because she wants to play

(B) because she loves apple pie

(C) because she didn't like her dad

(D) because she didn't want to clean her room

2. **Which is one reason Cassie decides she doesn't want to be invisible?**

(F) She loves to clean.

(G) Her mom misses her.

(H) She wouldn't get to hug her grandparents.

(J) She wants to be smart.

3. **Who is the main character in the story?**

(A) the dad

(B) Cassie

(C) the grandparents

(D) the teacher

4. **Why did the author write this story?**

(F) to give you information

(G) to get you to believe something

(H) to entertain you

(J) to explain how to do something

GO

Name _____   Date _____

DIRECTIONS: Read the story below. It tells about Sam being the oldest child in his family. Then, answer the questions.

The Oldest

Sometimes, Sam likes being the oldest. He can stay up one hour later. He can go places by himself. He also gets a bigger allowance for helping around the house. When his friend Brennan asks him to spend the night, Sam's mom says yes. He even gets to stay at his friend's house to eat dinner sometimes. Sam thinks it's great that he can read, ride a bike, and spell better than his brother. Sam's sister loves when he reads stories to her. Sam likes it, too. When his mom needs help cooking, she asks Sam, because he is the oldest.

Sometimes, Sam doesn't like being the oldest. He has to babysit his sister. She likes to go where he does. He also has to act more like a grown-up. Sam always has more jobs to do around the house. He has to help wash the dishes and take out the trash. His brother and sister get help when they have to clean their rooms. Sam doesn't get help. Sam doesn't like to be the oldest when his brother and sister want him to play with them all the time.

5. **What can Sam do better than his brother?**

- (A) play soccer
- (B) eat candy
- (C) ride a bike
- (D) watch movies

6. **What does Sam think about having to act more like a grown-up?**

- (F) He likes it.
- (G) He thinks his brother should act more grown-up.
- (H) It is one reason why he doesn't like to be the oldest.
- (J) He wants his parents to treat his brother like they treat him.

7. **Who is the main character in the story?**

- (A) Brennan
- (B) the sister
- (C) the brother
- (D) Sam

8. **Why did the author write this story?**

- (F) to give you information
- (G) to get you to believe something
- (H) to entertain you
- (J) to explain how to do something

STOP

Name _____   Date _____

English Language Arts

Understanding Nonfiction

Reading and Comprehension

DIRECTIONS: Read the paragraph below that tells how to make a peanut butter and jelly sandwich. Then, answer the questions.

How to Make a Peanut Butter and Jelly Sandwich

You will need peanut butter, jelly, and two pieces of bread. First, spread peanut butter on one piece of bread. Next, spread jelly on the other piece. Then, put the two pieces of bread together. Next, cut the sandwich in half. Finally, eat your sandwich and enjoy!

1. **What is the paragraph explaining?**

   Ⓐ how to make peanut butter

   Ⓑ how to cut a sandwich

   Ⓒ how to make a peanut butter and jelly sandwich

   Ⓓ how to put bread together

2. **What does the paragraph say to do after you spread peanut butter on one piece of bread?**

   Ⓕ cut the sandwich

   Ⓖ spread jelly on the other piece of bread

   Ⓗ put the two pieces together

   Ⓙ eat your sandwich and enjoy it

3. **What is the last step in the paragraph?**

   Ⓐ put the two pieces of bread together

   Ⓑ cut the sandwich

   Ⓒ eat and enjoy your sandwich

   Ⓓ spread peanut butter on one piece of bread

4. **Why did the author write this story?**

   Ⓕ to give you information

   Ⓖ to get you to believe something

   Ⓗ to entertain you

   Ⓙ to explain how to do something

GO

DIRECTIONS: Read the paragraph below that tells about dolphins and sharks. Then, answer the questions.

Dolphins and Sharks

Dolphins and sharks both live in the ocean, but they are very different. Dolphins are mammals. Sharks are fish. Both animals swim underwater. Sharks breathe through gills, and dolphins have lungs. Dolphins breathe through a blowhole on their heads. Dolphins give birth to live young. Sharks lay eggs. When the eggs hatch, young sharks come out. Sharks and dolphins live in water, but they have many differences.

5. **Which animal has lungs?**

   Ⓐ   a dolphin

   Ⓑ   a shark

   Ⓒ   a trout

   Ⓓ   a fish

6. **What do you learn about dolphins and sharks from this paragraph?**

   Ⓕ   They are mostly alike.

   Ⓖ   They both have blowholes.

   Ⓗ   There are many different things about them.

   Ⓙ   They live in rivers and streams.

7. **How are dolphins and sharks the same?**

   Ⓐ   They both lay eggs.

   Ⓑ   They both swim underwater.

   Ⓒ   They both breathe through gills.

   Ⓓ   They both are mammals.

8. **Why did the author write this story?**

   Ⓕ   to give you information

   Ⓖ   to get you to believe something

   Ⓗ   to entertain you

   Ⓙ   to explain how to do something

STOP

English Language Arts

| 1.0 |

Identifying Different Types of Text
Reading and Comprehension

DIRECTIONS: Read the passage. Then, answer the questions.

Amusement Park Opens
July 2, 2007
John Smith, *Herald Journal* **reporter**

Kelly's Grove, normally open only for family picnics, will be open to the public on July 4. The park offers sixteen rides, including two roller coasters. It also has games, miniature golf, food stands, picnic tables, and a water park. Fireworks are planned for the end of the evening. Plan to bring your family for a fun-filled day.

1. **Where would you most likely find this information?**
   - (A) in an advertisement
   - (B) on a sign
   - (C) in a newspaper
   - (D) in an encyclopedia

2. **What is the headline of this story?**
   - (F) July 2, 2007
   - (G) Amusement Park Opens
   - (H) Fun and Fireworks
   - (J) Kelly's Grove

3. **What is the purpose of this passage?**
   - (A) to entertain the reader
   - (B) to get the reader to believe something
   - (C) to give the reader information
   - (D) to explain how to do something

DIRECTIONS: Choose the best answer.

4. **The purpose of an encyclopedia is to _____ .**
   - (F) give definitions and spellings of words
   - (G) provide maps of different places
   - (H) give information about recent or upcoming events in the area and world
   - (J) provide information and facts about different topics

5. **The purpose of a dictionary is to _____ .**
   - (A) give definitions and spellings of words
   - (B) provide maps of different places
   - (C) give information about recent or upcoming events in the area and world
   - (D) provide information and facts about different topics

6. **The purpose of an atlas is to _____ .**
   - (F) give definitions and spellings of words
   - (G) provide maps of different places
   - (H) give information about recent or upcoming events in the area and world
   - (J) provide information and facts about different topics

7. **The purpose of a newspaper is to _____ .**
   - (A) give definitions and spellings of words
   - (B) provide maps of different places
   - (C) give information about recent or upcoming events in the area and world
   - (D) provide information and facts about different topics

GO

8. **Where would you look to check the spelling of *elephant*?**

    (F) in a newspaper

    (G) in an atlas

    (H) in a dictionary

    (J) in an encyclopedia

9. **Where would you look to find information about turtles?**

    (A) in a newspaper

    (B) in an atlas

    (C) in an encyclopedia

    (D) in a dictionary

10. **Where would you look to find a map of Texas?**

    (F) in a newspaper

    (G) in an atlas

    (H) in a dictionary

    (J) in an encyclopedia

11. **Where would you look to find yesterday's sports scores?**

    (A) in a newspaper

    (B) in an atlas

    (C) in an encyclopedia

    (D) in a dictionary

DIRECTIONS: A table of contents gives you the names of chapters or topics in a book. Read the table of contents. Then, answer the questions.

TABLE OF CONTENTS

Chapter 1: Choosing Your Breed of Dog. . . . 11

Chapter 2: Selecting the Right Puppy 42

Chapter 3: Care and Feeding of Puppies . . . 58

Chapter 4: Training Young Dogs 86

Chapter 5: Medical Care for Dogs. 102

Chapter 6: Do You Have a Champion? 116

---

12. **Which chapter starts on page 42?**

    (F) Chapter 1

    (G) Chapter 2

    (H) Chapter 3

    (J) Chapter 4

13. **The chapter titled "Training Young Dogs" starts on which page?**

    (A) 11

    (B) 42

    (C) 58

    (D) 86

14. **Which chapter tells you how to care for your puppy?**

    (F) Chapter 1

    (G) Chapter 2

    (H) Chapter 3

    (J) Chapter 6

STOP

English Language Arts

2.0

Identifying Genres

Reading and Comprehension

DIRECTIONS: Read the story and answer the questions.

The White Spaceship

One night in the woods, I saw a bright, white spaceship under some trees. I was scared, but I tried to be brave. I was afraid the aliens might take me away to their planet. Suddenly, the spaceship opened, and a girl stepped out. She had green skin and three eyes.

Clue A **genre** is a kind of writing. A story is fiction if the people and events are made-up, or not real. Writing is nonfiction if the people and events are real.

1. **This story is which genre (type) of writing?**
   - Ⓐ poetry
   - Ⓑ fiction
   - Ⓒ biography
   - Ⓓ nonfiction

2. **Which clue in the story helped you decide what genre it is?**
   - Ⓕ The spaceship is really a camper.
   - Ⓖ The girl is an alien.
   - Ⓗ The aliens fly away again.
   - Ⓙ The speaker is having a dream.

3. **This genre is usually about _____ .**
   - Ⓐ the life of a real person
   - Ⓑ how something came to be the way it is
   - Ⓒ how to do something
   - Ⓓ made-up places and events

4. **The purpose of this genre is usually to _____ .**
   - Ⓕ entertain the reader
   - Ⓖ get the reader to believe something
   - Ⓗ give the reader information
   - Ⓙ explain to the reader how to do something

GO

Name _____ Date _____

DIRECTIONS: Read the paragraph below that tells about horses. Then, answer the questions.

Horses

Horses are beautiful animals. Most horses have smooth, shiny coats. They have long manes and tails. Their hair may be brown, black, white, yellow, or spotted. Sometimes, horses neigh, or make a loud, long cry. Horses need to be brushed every day. This helps keep them clean. Many people keep horses as pets or to work on farms. Some people enjoy riding them for fun. Horses are wonderful animals.

5. **This story is which genre (type) of writing?**

   (A) poetry

   (B) biography

   (C) fiction

   (D) nonfiction

6. **Which clues in the story helped you decide what genre it is?**

   (F) The author likes horses.

   (G) Facts about horses are given.

   (H) There is a picture of a horse.

   (J) Horses are wonderful animals.

7. **The purpose of this genre is usually to _____ .**

   (A) entertain the reader

   (B) get the reader to believe something

   (C) give the reader information

   (D) explain to the reader how to do something

8. **This genre usually includes _____ .**

   (F) true information

   (G) cartoon characters

   (H) made-up places and events

   (J) words that rhyme

STOP

English Language Arts

2.0

Identifying Characteristics of Stories
Reading and Comprehension

DIRECTIONS: Read the story. Then, answer the questions.

Lazy Time

Sally and Ned are swaying slowly in the family swing. The air is crisp. Sally puts her arm around Ned and snuggles into his shaggy body. Ned's tongue licks Sally's hand that lies on her blue-jeaned leg. They watch a slow ladybug crawl underneath a pile of old, brown leaves. One red leaf drifts to the top of the ladybug's leaf pile. Ned's graying ears stand up as a *V* of geese honks goodbye. The sky slowly turns from blue, to pink, to purple, to black.

The first star shines as Sally's mom calls her in to eat. Sally gives a last push as she slides out of the swing. She walks to the back door of the house. Ned leaps down. He barks once at a rabbit, and then chases after Sally. She smiles and rubs Ned's head as they walk into the warm house together.

1. **The setting is _____ .**
   - Ⓐ the main problem in a story
   - Ⓑ where and when a story takes place
   - Ⓒ the reason the author wrote a story
   - Ⓓ the picture with a story

2. **This story most likely takes place in _____ .**
   - Ⓕ a made-up time
   - Ⓖ the past
   - Ⓗ the present
   - Ⓙ the future

3. **What time of year is it?**
   - Ⓐ summer
   - Ⓑ fall
   - Ⓒ winter
   - Ⓓ spring

4. **What time of day is it?**
   - Ⓕ morning
   - Ⓖ lunchtime
   - Ⓗ afternoon
   - Ⓙ evening

5. **What meal is Sally's family going to eat?**
   - Ⓐ breakfast
   - Ⓑ lunch
   - Ⓒ snack
   - Ⓓ dinner

6. **Who is the main character?**
   - Ⓕ Sally
   - Ⓖ Ned
   - Ⓗ the ladybug
   - Ⓙ Sally's mom

STOP

English Language Arts

3.0

Using Letter-Sound Correspondence

Reading and Comprehension

DIRECTIONS: Choose the best answer.

Example:

Which word has the same beginning sound as *sheep*?

- (A) chin
- (B) shake
- (C) seven
- (D) sleep

Answer: (B)

Clue Read all the answer choices before choosing the one you think is correct.

1. **Which word has the same beginning sound as** *blue*?

   - (A) blast
   - (B) boy
   - (C) brush
   - (D) few

2. **Which word has the same vowel sound as** *join*?

   - (F) tool
   - (G) joke
   - (H) spoil
   - (J) cold

3. **Which word has the same ending sound as** *from*?

   - (A) float
   - (B) barn
   - (C) come
   - (D) fry

4. **Which word has the same vowel sound as** *found*?

   - (F) down
   - (G) flood
   - (H) road
   - (J) pan

5. **Which word has the same ending sound as** *spend*?

   - (A) seen
   - (B) pound
   - (C) pain
   - (D) spot

6. **Which word has the same beginning sound as** *another*?

   - (F) about
   - (G) arm
   - (H) clue
   - (J) ace

GO

Name _____ Date _____

DIRECTIONS: Choose the best answer.

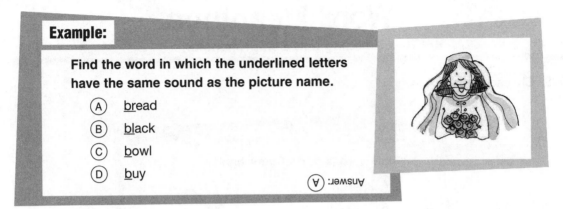

Example:

Find the word in which the underlined letters have the same sound as the picture name.

- (A) bread
- (B) black
- (C) bowl
- (D) buy

Answer: (A)

Clue Repeat the directions to yourself as you look at the answer choices.

7. **Find the word that has the same beginning sound as the picture name.**

- (A) frame
- (B) flame
- (C) fork
- (D) farm

8. **Find the word that has the same ending sound as the picture name.**

- (F) meant
- (G) stand
- (H) earn
- (J) barn

9. **Look at the word in the box. Find the other word that has the same vowel sound as the underlined part.**

float

- (A) block
- (B) board
- (C) coat
- (D) pool

10. **Look at the word in the box. Find the other word that has the same vowel sound as the underlined part.**

door

- (F) knock
- (G) open
- (H) window
- (J) chore

STOP

Identifying Word Meanings
Reading and Comprehension

DIRECTIONS: Choose the best answer.

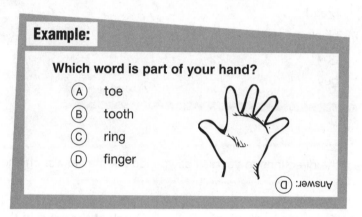

Example:

Which word is part of your hand?

(A) toe

(B) tooth

(C) ring

(D) finger

Answer: (D)

 Clue   Key words in the question will help you find the answer.

1. Which word is something that flies?

(A) bird

(B) cat

(C) worm

(D) dog

2. Which word means *to leave*?

(F) enter

(G) grow

(H) exit

(J) stay

3. Which word means *to finish*?

(A) finally

(B) different

(C) start

(D) complete

4. Which word means *to start*?

(F) read

(G) begin

(H) end

(J) done

5. Which word is something you drive on?

(A) shoes

(B) road

(C) stop

(D) door

6. Which word is where a worm lives?

(F) ground

(G) nest

(H) house

(J) car

STOP

Name _____   Date _____

3.0

Using Words with Multiple Meanings
Reading and Comprehension

DIRECTIONS: Some words have more than one meaning. Choose the word that will make sense in both blanks.

Example:

Let's _____ outside.

She bumped her _____ when she fell.

- (A) went
- (B) leg
- (C) self
- (D) head

Answer: (D)

 Clue Remember, the correct answer must make sense in both blanks.

1. _____ the light over here.

   The _____ on this pencil broke.

   - (A) point
   - (B) eraser
   - (C) shine
   - (D) top

2. The boat began to _____ .

   Dad washed the dishes in the _____ .

   - (F) wait
   - (G) tub
   - (H) sink
   - (J) pan

3. Hit the _____ with the hammer.

   The _____ on my little finger is broken.

   - (A) tack
   - (B) nail
   - (C) skin
   - (D) wood

4. Did you _____ your visitor well?

   My dog loves to get a _____ from me.

   - (F) feed
   - (G) snack
   - (H) enjoy
   - (J) treat

5. The brown _____ was sleeping in the cave.

   She could not _____ to hear any more scary stories.

   - (A) hear
   - (B) fox
   - (C) bear
   - (D) take

STOP

English Language Arts

3.0

Using Context Clues

Reading and Comprehension

DIRECTIONS: Choose the word that best fits in the blank.

Examples:

The ____(A)____ was easy to enter. All you had to do was go to the park. To win, you had to ____(B)____ how many jelly beans were in the jar.

A.
- Ⓐ door
- Ⓑ contest
- Ⓒ tunnel
- Ⓓ house

Answer: (B)

B.
- Ⓕ guess
- Ⓖ read
- Ⓗ count
- Ⓙ sing

Answer: (F)

Clue

When deciding which answer is best, try each answer choice in the blank.

Each house on the block had a ____(1)____ backyard. Each had small patches of lawn and flowers. Some even had ____(2)____ gardens.

1.
- Ⓐ unlikely
- Ⓑ neat
- Ⓒ lost
- Ⓓ firm

2.
- Ⓕ sand
- Ⓖ problem
- Ⓗ vegetable
- Ⓙ blanket

One morning, Chris couldn't ____(3)____ his homework. He looked on his ____(4)____ , but it wasn't there. He wondered, "Where could it be?"

3.
- Ⓐ find
- Ⓑ hidden
- Ⓒ hear
- Ⓓ friend

4.
- Ⓕ lamp
- Ⓖ dog
- Ⓗ desk
- Ⓙ sock

STOP

Name _____ Date _____

3.0

Picture Comprehension

Reading and Comprehension

DIRECTIONS: Look at the picture. Then, choose the word that best fits in the blank.

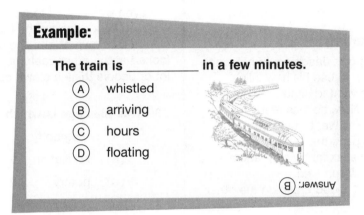

Example:

The train is _____ in a few minutes.

- (A) whistled
- (B) arriving
- (C) hours
- (D) floating

Answer: (B)

Clue

Look back at the picture when you choose an answer to fit in the blank.

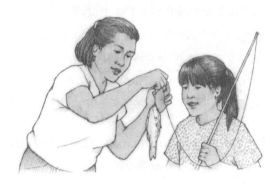

1. **The line for the movie _____ around the corner.**

- (A) went
- (B) ran
- (C) skipped
- (D) sang

2. **This was a film that everyone wanted to _____ .**

- (F) like
- (G) hear
- (H) see
- (J) drink

3. **Jenna caught small fish with her new fishing _____ .**

- (A) bait
- (B) camp
- (C) box
- (D) rod

4. **Her _____ helped her take it off the hook.**

- (F) mom
- (G) dad
- (H) baby
- (J) brother

STOP

Name _____ Date _____

Mini-Test 1

Reading and Comprehension

DIRECTIONS: Read the stories. Then, answer the questions.

Skating

It was a sunny, spring day. Jason could not wait for Tasha to show him how to use his new inline skates. Jason had always wanted skates. He finally got them for his birthday. Now, he was ready for his first lesson. Jason and Tasha went to the park.

When they got to the park, they saw Michael. Michael raced by the slower skaters and made a face at them. "Show-off," Jason said.

Suddenly, Jason heard a loud crash on the other side of the park.

"What was that?" asked Tasha.

Michael limped around the corner. He was covered with twigs and leaves.

"I don't think we have to worry about show-offs anymore," Jason said with a smile.

1. **What is the setting for the story?**

    (A) outside on a bright spring day

    (B) inside on a cold winter day

    (C) inside on a chilly spring day

    (D) outside on a cool fall day

2. **Who are the two main characters in the story?**

    (F) Michael and Tasha

    (G) Jason and Michael

    (H) Jason and Tasha

    (J) the skates

The Party

Lynn was invited to a costume party. There was going to be a prize for the funniest costume. Lynn went as a clown. When she got to the party, she looked at the other costumes. Lynn said, "I guess a lot of people think a clown costume is funny!"

3. **This passage is which genre (type) of writing?**

    (A) biography

    (B) nonfiction

    (C) poetry

    (D) fiction

4. **Why did the author write this story?**

    (F) to give you information

    (G) to get you to believe something

    (H) to entertain you

    (J) to explain how to do something

5. **Why does Lynn guess that a lot of people think clown costumes are funny?**

    (A) Many people at the party are dressed up like clowns.

    (B) Lynn likes clowns.

    (C) Lynn says everyone should dress like a clown.

    (D) No one else at the party dressed like a clown.

GO

Name _____ Date _____

DIRECTIONS: For numbers 6 and 7, choose the word that best fits in the blank.

Matt and Alan ____(6)____ to the top of the tall hill. They laid down in the ____(7)____ grass and watched the clouds.

6.   (F)   raced

     (G)   picked

     (H)   took

     (J)   swam

7.   (A)   stop

     (B)   round

     (C)   winter

     (D)   soft

DIRECTIONS: Choose the best answer.

8. **Where would you look to find out how _yesterday_ is broken into syllables?**

     (F)   in a newspaper

     (G)   in an atlas

     (H)   in a dictionary

     (J)   in an encyclopedia

9. **Where would you look to find a map of Oregon?**

     (A)   in a newspaper

     (B)   in an atlas

     (C)   in a dictionary

     (D)   in an encyclopedia

DIRECTIONS: Choose the best answer to each question.

10. **Which word has the same ending sound as _build_?**

     (F)   bell

     (G)   cold

     (H)   heart

     (J)   bring

11. **Which word has the same vowel sound as _bread_?**

     (A)   round

     (B)   rest

     (C)   meet

     (D)   does

12. **Which word means _to lift up_?**

     (F)   find

     (G)   raise

     (H)   release

     (J)   haul

13. **Which word is part of a tree?**

     (A)   shade

     (B)   cool

     (C)   leaf

     (D)   moist

STOP

English Language Arts

4.0

Building Vocabulary

Writing

DIRECTIONS: Choose the word that best matches the picture.

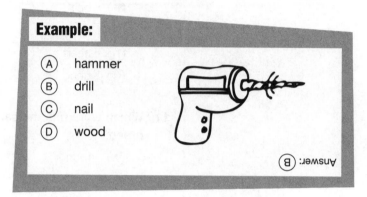

Example:

- (A) hammer
- (B) drill
- (C) nail
- (D) wood

Answer: (B)

 Clue   Look at the picture carefully, and then read the choices.

1.
- (A) smell
- (B) feel
- (C) hear
- (D) see

3.
- (A) leaf
- (B) wood
- (C) branch
- (D) tree

2.
- (F) clap
- (G) shake
- (H) touch
- (J) snap

4.
- (F) watering
- (G) smoking
- (H) steaming
- (J) cooking

GO

Name _____ Date _____

DIRECTIONS: Choose the word that best fits in the blanks.

Clue When picking the best answer, try each answer choice in the blank.

Our neighbor is a gardener. One of her
_____**(5)**_____ trees died last week. She said it was
because of a bug that likes to eat _____**(6)**_____ .

5. Ⓐ girl
  Ⓑ half
  Ⓒ small
  Ⓓ corner

6. Ⓕ each
  Ⓖ leaves
  Ⓗ dirt
  Ⓙ tender

One sunny June day, a man _____**(7)**_____ too fast
down the road. A police officer stopped him and gave
him a _____**(8)**_____ .

7. Ⓐ drove
  Ⓑ walked
  Ⓒ paced
  Ⓓ ran

8. Ⓕ picture
  Ⓖ hat
  Ⓗ rest
  Ⓙ ticket

**9. There are many different _____ of bats.
One kind is the brown bat.**
  Ⓐ only
  Ⓑ paper
  Ⓒ kinds
  Ⓓ items

**10. _____ brown bats eat insects. One bat
can eat 600 mosquitoes in just one hour.**
  Ⓕ Second
  Ⓖ Little
  Ⓗ Sleep
  Ⓙ Trip

11. Nate wanted to _____ more about bats.
  Ⓐ play
  Ⓑ pick
  Ⓒ scared
  Ⓓ learn

STOP

English Language Arts

4.0

Synonyms

Writing

DIRECTIONS: Look at the underlined word in each sentence. Which word is a synonym for that word?

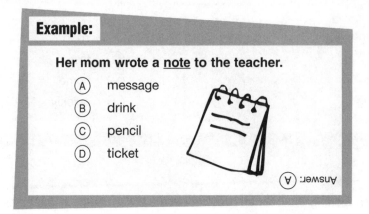

Example:

Her mom wrote a <u>note</u> to the teacher.

- (A) message
- (B) drink
- (C) pencil
- (D) ticket

Answer: (A)

 Synonyms are words that have the same meaning. *Fast* and *quick* are synonyms.

---

1. **Susan was <u>grateful</u> that her dad drove her to school.**
   - (A) thankful
   - (B) busy
   - (C) angry
   - (D) finished

2. **The brothers <u>yelled</u> for their dog to come home.**
   - (F) cared
   - (G) called
   - (H) heard
   - (J) whispered

3. **Grandma asked me to <u>split</u> the cookies evenly between the children.**
   - (A) use
   - (B) think
   - (C) divide
   - (D) stand

4. **I always keep my room very <u>neat</u>.**
   - (F) bad
   - (G) pretty
   - (H) tidy
   - (J) dark

5. **She likes to eat <u>big</u> oranges.**
   - (A) large
   - (B) tiny
   - (C) ready
   - (D) round

6. **She watched the cat <u>jump</u> off the chair.**
   - (F) leap
   - (G) lick
   - (H) break
   - (J) dream

STOP

English Language Arts

4.0

Antonyms

Writing

DIRECTIONS: Look at the underlined word in each sentence. Choose the word that is the antonym of the underlined word.

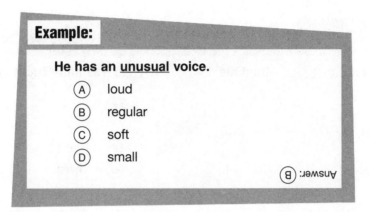

Example:

He has an <u>unusual</u> voice.

- (A) loud
- (B) regular
- (C) soft
- (D) small

Answer: (B)

Clue

Antonyms are words that have opposite meanings. *Forward* and *backward* are antonyms.

1. They drove down the <u>narrow</u> road.
   - (A) long
   - (B) new
   - (C) bumpy
   - (D) wide

2. She picked her <u>fancy</u> dress to wear to the party.
   - (F) best
   - (G) plain
   - (H) small
   - (J) little

3. She made sure the knot was good and <u>tight</u>.
   - (A) clean
   - (B) different
   - (C) loose
   - (D) last

4. <u>After</u> granting our three wishes, the kind genie vanished from sight.
   - (F) before
   - (G) asked
   - (H) going
   - (J) got

5. He thought his bike was <u>fast</u>.
   - (A) funny
   - (B) food
   - (C) last
   - (D) slow

6. On Thursday, Daniel was <u>absent</u>.
   - (F) giving
   - (G) present
   - (H) hurt
   - (J) gone

STOP

English Language Arts

4.0

Word Usage

Writing

DIRECTIONS: Look at the sentence. Which word or phrase should go in the blank or could replace the underlined part?

Examples:

A. He makes friends _____ than his brother.

- (A) easy
- (B) easiest
- (C) easily
- (D) easier

Answer: D

B. <u>Suki</u> was more frightened than Jawan.

- (F) Its
- (G) She
- (H) Her
- (J) Them

Answer: G

 Clue Your first answer is usually right.

1. Leah is the _____ at math.
   - (A) better
   - (B) good
   - (C) best
   - (D) well

2. Aunt Jeanne is the _____ teacher I know.
   - (F) finest
   - (G) fine
   - (H) finer
   - (J) finally

3. Hunter likes to draw _____ than his sister does.
   - (A) most
   - (B) best
   - (C) bestest
   - (D) more

4. The movie that <u>Sam and Amy</u> watched was very funny.
   - (F) he
   - (G) they
   - (H) them
   - (J) us

5. We found <u>the shoe</u> in the bottom of the box.
   - (A) me
   - (B) there
   - (C) she
   - (D) it

6. Please help <u>your brother</u> clean his room.
   - (F) her
   - (G) we
   - (H) him
   - (J) it

STOP

English Language Arts

5.0

Writing with Focus

Writing

DIRECTIONS: Read the paragraph. Then, answer the questions that follow.

Example:

Ben and Troy visited the city zoo. The bears and lions were asleep. Troy fed peanuts to an elephant. Ben rode a pony.

Which sentence would belong in the paragraph?

- (A) Ben rode a fast ride at the amusement park.
- (B) Ben and Troy had a great day at the zoo.
- (C) Ben and Troy went to the baseball game.
- (D) Troy went to his friend's house.

Answer: (B)

 Clue A paragraph should focus on one idea. All the sentences in a paragraph should be related.

Dear Aunt Elida,

You will never believe what happened yesterday! I was walking down the street when a fire truck went by me. I followed the truck. It went to my best friend Coby's house. Coby was outside with his family. Their house had caught on fire. Because they had practiced fire drills, they made it out safely. The firefighters put out the fire. The kitchen was the only room damaged. Coby and his family are doing fine.

Love, Chantal

1. Which sentence would not belong in this paragraph?

- (A) I went to get ice cream.
- (B) Coby was upset about the fire.
- (C) Coby's mom and dad said everything would be fine.
- (D) The smoke was really thick.

2. Which sentence would belong in this paragraph?

- (F) Firefighters wear helmets.
- (G) The firefighters that helped Coby were great.
- (H) Coby's family is going on a trip to Colorado.
- (J) I read a book about firefighters.

English Language Arts

| 5.0 |

Completing Sentences

Writing

DIRECTIONS: Read the sentence. Which phrase completes the sentence?

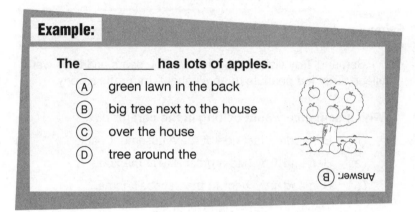

Example:

The _____ has lots of apples.

- (A) green lawn in the back
- (B) big tree next to the house
- (C) over the house
- (D) tree around the

Answer: (B)

Clue

If you are not sure which answer is correct, take your best guess. Get rid of answer choices you know are wrong.

1. You need a ticket _____ .

- (A) to fly in a plane
- (B) to bake
- (C) to drive in the street
- (D) in the row

2. _____ took place last Saturday.

- (F) Dogs and cats
- (G) Sunny day
- (H) The picnic
- (J) Running feet

3. Alexis and her dog, Boots, like to run and _____ .

- (A) around the bush
- (B) leaving on the hat
- (C) with the other children
- (D) play at the park

4. Tony is the boy who _____ .

- (F) eating the cookies
- (G) takes his time doing his homework
- (H) until he stops running
- (J) needing to go to sleep

5. I put _____ and went for a ride.

- (A) answer my mom
- (B) around the corner
- (C) on my bike helmet
- (D) for my birthday gift

6. Dan walked _____ each day.

- (F) along five miles to
- (G) leaving his jacket
- (H) so mom would
- (J) one mile to school

STOP

English Language Arts

| 5.0 |

Identifying
Complete Sentences
Writing

DIRECTIONS: Read each choice. Which one is a complete sentence?

Example:

Ⓐ   This is my book.

Ⓑ   These there clocks set wrong.

Ⓒ   Who going to the wedding?

Ⓓ   Where she gone?

Answer: Ⓐ

Clue — A complete sentence has a subject and a verb. It says a complete idea.

1. Ⓐ   On the light.
    Ⓑ   Went down the hill.
    Ⓒ   She ate the candy.
    Ⓓ   Pink and blue ribbons.

2. Ⓕ   Picked from the tree.
    Ⓖ   See the boy and girl.
    Ⓗ   The picnic.
    Ⓙ   Natalie rolled in the sand.

3. Ⓐ   Minka sat in the sun.
    Ⓑ   She to go school.
    Ⓒ   Dad cookies and cakes to eat.
    Ⓓ   Miss Read likes when her students.

4. Ⓕ   My wagon in the garage.
    Ⓖ   Your brother went with you.
    Ⓗ   Juliet saw what she knew was.
    Ⓙ   Mary Ella and felt like she had a fever.

5. Ⓐ   The family had fun at the circus.
    Ⓑ   The children cried and wanted lots of.
    Ⓒ   She the keys to the car.
    Ⓓ   Arleen color is black.

6. Ⓕ   Feet, toes, and knees.
    Ⓖ   How she like to?
    Ⓗ   The red balloon was still in her hand.
    Ⓙ   Won the prize last night at the birthday party.

STOP

English Language Arts

5.0

Identifying the Main Idea
Writing

DIRECTIONS: Read the passage. Then, answer the questions that follow.

Example:

At 5:00 P.M., we were called to the home of a Mr. and Mrs. Bear. They found that the lock on their front door had been forced open. Food had been stolen and a chair was broken. Baby Bear then went upstairs and found someone asleep in his bed.

What is the main idea of this paragraph?

Ⓐ Someone broke a lock.

Ⓑ Someone stole some food.

Ⓒ Mr. and Mrs. Bear's house was broken into.

Ⓓ Baby Bear found his bed.

Answer: Ⓒ

 Clue The **main idea** is the most important message of a paragraph or story.

Pioneer Diary

Today, we left our dear home in Ohio forever. Soon, we will be a thousand miles away. The distance is too great for us to ever return. Oh, how Grandmother cried as we said goodbye! Uncle Dan and Aunt Martha have bought our farm, so it is no longer our home. All we have now is what is here in our wagon.

When we drove past the woods at the edge of our fields, Papa said to me, "Ellen, take a good look at those trees. It will be many years before we see big trees like that again. We will have to plant trees on the prairie." I felt like crying, just like Grandmother, but I wanted to show Papa that I could be brave.

1. **What is the main idea of this story?**

    Ⓐ Ellen feels like crying.

    Ⓑ Ellen wants to be brave.

    Ⓒ Ellen and her father are moving to the prairie.

    Ⓓ Ellen's father has sold his farm.

2. **How do you know where Ellen is moving?**

    Ⓕ Her grandmother cries.

    Ⓖ Her father says they will have to plant trees on the prairie.

    Ⓗ Her father has packed a wagon.

    Ⓙ Ellen is keeping a diary.

3. **Why does Ellen say she is leaving "forever"?**

    Ⓐ In pioneer days, people were not allowed to come back home again.

    Ⓑ In pioneer days, the trip out West was thousands and thousands of miles.

    Ⓒ In pioneer days, it was too far for people to travel back and forth for visits.

    Ⓓ In pioneer days, people did not sell their farms.

Name _____   Date _____

Identifying Supporting Details
Writing

DIRECTIONS: Read the passage. Then, use the passage to fill in the topic sentence below. Fill in the rest of the ovals with supporting details.

Insects in Winter

In the summertime, insects can be seen buzzing and fluttering around us. But as winter's cold weather begins, the insects seem to disappear. Do you know where they go? Many insects find a warm place to spend the winter.

Ants try to dig deep into the ground. Some beetles stack up in piles under rocks or dead leaves.

Female grasshoppers do not even stay around for winter. In the fall, they lay their eggs and die. The eggs hatch in the spring.

Bees also try to protect themselves from the winter cold. Honeybees gather in a ball in the middle of their hive. The bees stay in this tight ball trying to stay warm.

Winter is very hard for insects, but each spring the survivors come out, and the buzzing and fluttering begin again.

 Supporting details help to explain the main idea of the passage.

Many insects find a _____ place to spend the _____ .

STOP

English Language Arts

| 6.0 |

Spelling

Writing

DIRECTIONS: Read the sentences. Which word fits in the sentence and is spelled <u>correctly</u>?

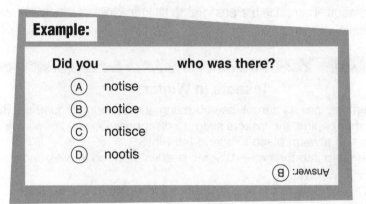

Example:

Did you _____ who was there?

- (A) notise
- (B) notice
- (C) notisce
- (D) nootis

Answer: (B)

If a question is too difficult, skip it and move on to another one. Come back later to the question you skipped.

1. The lake is _____ that hill.
   - (A) beayond
   - (B) beyon
   - (C) beyond
   - (D) beyont

2. Be _____ near the pond.
   - (F) carefull
   - (G) cairful
   - (H) carful
   - (J) careful

3. She went to the pool _____ she wanted to swim.
   - (A) becuz
   - (B) because
   - (C) beecus
   - (D) becuas

4. Do you _____ which way the twins went?
   - (F) kno
   - (G) noow
   - (H) kow
   - (J) know

5. She was sure the teacher would stop the _____ .
   - (A) fight
   - (B) fiet
   - (C) figt
   - (D) fieat

6. The spinner _____ stopped on the red space.
   - (F) fineally
   - (G) finally
   - (H) fineulee
   - (J) finelly

GO

Name _____ Date _____

DIRECTIONS: Read the sentences. Look at the underlined words. Which one is not spelled <u>correctly</u>?

Example:

<u>Our</u> <u>dailly</u> run is <u>about</u> two miles.

Ⓐ   Ⓑ   Ⓒ

Answer: Ⓑ

Clue If you are not sure which answer is correct, take your best guess. Rule out answer choices you know are spelled correctly.

7. We <u>usuelly</u> arrive <u>around</u> <u>three</u> o'clock.
       Ⓐ   Ⓑ Ⓒ

8. <u>Did</u> you <u>forgit</u> <u>your</u> hat?
  Ⓕ   Ⓖ Ⓗ

9. Dad <u>grilld</u> <u>some</u> corn for <u>dinner</u>.
    Ⓐ Ⓑ   Ⓒ

10. Call Mom <u>aftr</u> you get <u>home</u> <u>tomorrow</u>.
      Ⓕ   Ⓖ   Ⓗ

11. Do you like to <u>build</u> sand <u>castles</u> when you are at the <u>beech</u>?
            Ⓐ   Ⓑ   Ⓒ

12. Jake's bus was ten <u>minutes</u> <u>laat</u> <u>today</u>.
         Ⓕ   Ⓖ Ⓗ

STOP

English Language Arts

6.0

Capitalization

Writing

DIRECTIONS: Which word in the sentence needs to be capitalized?

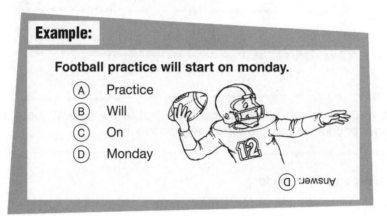

Example:

Football practice will start on monday.

- Ⓐ Practice
- Ⓑ Will
- Ⓒ On
- Ⓓ Monday

Answer: Ⓓ

Clue Sentences begin with capital letters. Important words in a sentence begin with capital letters.

---

1. **My friends will visit us on thanksgiving.**
   - Ⓐ Friends
   - Ⓑ Visit
   - Ⓒ Us
   - Ⓓ Thanksgiving

2. **Jake is going to the movies with his family on saturday.**
   - Ⓕ Going
   - Ⓖ Movies
   - Ⓗ Saturday
   - Ⓙ Family

3. **Donald and gordy like to visit Brook Manor.**
   - Ⓐ Gordy
   - Ⓑ Like
   - Ⓒ To
   - Ⓓ Visit

4. **Lily lived in Mexico, but now she lives in the United States of america.**
   - Ⓕ Lived
   - Ⓖ But
   - Ⓗ Lives
   - Ⓙ America

5. **Marisa went to ohio to go shopping.**
   - Ⓐ Went
   - Ⓑ To
   - Ⓒ Ohio
   - Ⓓ Shopping

6. **her favorite animal to visit at the zoo is the kangaroo.**
   - Ⓕ Her
   - Ⓖ Favorite
   - Ⓗ Animal
   - Ⓙ Zoo

STOP

Name _____   Date _____

6.0

Punctuation

Writing

DIRECTIONS: Read the sentences. Choose the correct punctuation mark that is needed.

Examples:

A. The phone is ringing

- (A) .
- (B) !
- (C) ?
- (D) none

Answer: (A)

Donald takes Dudley to the store to buy a big bag of dog food. Each dog food maker says that his dog food is the <u>best</u>

(B)

B. (F) best?

(G) best.

(H) best!

Answer: (H)

Clue

Saying each sentence to yourself can help you decide which punctuation mark is needed.

1. Watch out

- (A) ?
- (B) .
- (C) !
- (D) none

2. What do you think Mom will buy at the grocery store

- (F) .
- (G) ?
- (H) !
- (J) none

3. The Carls family moved into the neighborhood

- (A) !
- (B) ?
- (C) .
- (D) none

4. Where is Nicky going with her ball

- (F) ?
- (G) .
- (H) !
- (J) none

The window was open in the <u>kitchen</u> When it started

(5)

to rain, I ran close to it. I got there just in time. Wow,

it rained a <u>lot</u>

(6)

5. (A) kitchen!

(B) kitchen?

(C) kitchen.

6. (F) lot?

(G) lot!

(H) lot.

STOP

English Language Arts

6.0

Contractions

Writing

DIRECTIONS: Look at each of the words. Choose the answer that shows what the contraction means.

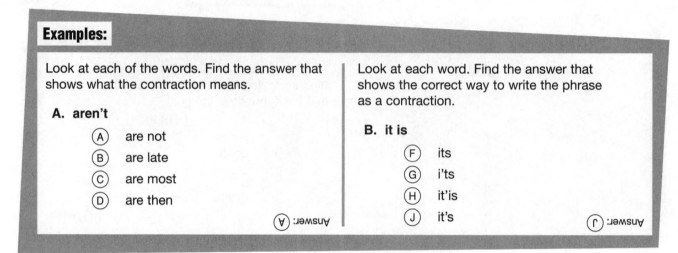

Examples:

Look at each of the words. Find the answer that shows what the contraction means.

A. aren't

- (A) are not
- (B) are late
- (C) are most
- (D) are then

Answer: (A)

Look at each word. Find the answer that shows the correct way to write the phrase as a contraction.

B. it is

- (F) its
- (G) i'ts
- (H) it'is
- (J) it's

Answer: (J)

1. don't

- (A) did it
- (B) drive in
- (C) do think
- (D) do not

2. they're

- (F) they rest
- (G) they are
- (H) they run
- (J) they care

3. she'll

- (A) she falls
- (B) she all
- (C) she will
- (D) she likes

DIRECTIONS: Look at each word. Choose the answer that shows the correct way to write the phrase as a contraction.

4. we are

- (F) we're
- (G) wer'e
- (H) we'ar
- (J) wear

5. he would

- (A) he'ld
- (B) he'd
- (C) hewo'd
- (D) he w'd

6. cannot

- (F) cano't
- (G) cant
- (H) can't
- (J) cann't

STOP

English Language Arts

| 4.0–6.0 |

For pages 24–38

Mini-Test 2

Writing

DIRECTIONS: Read the passage. Then, answer questions 1 and 2.

People who may not be able to hear or speak well use sign language. They use their hands instead of their voices to talk. Their hands make signals to show different letters, words, and ideas. For example, to say the word *love,* cross your arms over your chest.

Other people use sign language, too. Have you ever watched a football game? The referees use hand signals to let you know what has happened in the game, such as a foul or time out. Have you ever watched a police officer direct traffic? The police officer can use sign language to tell cars to stop and go.

Guess who else uses sign language? You! You wave your hand when you say *hello* and *good-bye.* You nod your head up and down to say *yes.* You shake your head back and forth to say *no.* You use your fingers to point and show which way to go. We use our hands and body to make signals all of the time!

1. **What is the main idea of the story?**
   - (A) using sign language
   - (B) writing sign language
   - (C) playing with children who use sign language
   - (D) buying food using sign language

2. **Which of the following details does not support the main idea of this story?**
   - (F) People use their hands to make signals for different words, letters, and ideas.
   - (G) The police officer can use sign language to tell cars to stop and go.
   - (H) We use our hands and body to make signals all of the time!
   - (J) Very few people use sign language.

DIRECTIONS: Choose the best answer.

3. **Which word is a synonym for the underlined word in the following sentence?**

   She knew where the hidden key was kept.
   - (A) open
   - (B) known
   - (C) friendly
   - (D) secret

4. **Which word is an antonym for the underlined word in the following sentence?**

   Amarra's doctor said she was healthy.
   - (F) wound
   - (G) heal
   - (H) sick
   - (J) find

5. **We made the _____ snowman on our street.**
   - (A) biggest
   - (B) bigger
   - (C) most big
   - (D) most biggest

6. **Which word can replace the underlined words in the following sentence?**

   Micah and Ben ran past my house.
   - (F) He
   - (G) They
   - (H) Them
   - (J) Us

GO

Name _____   Date _____

DIRECTIONS: Read the words carefully. Choose the word that is not spelled correctly.

7. (A) hidden

    (B) never

    (C) chaire

    (D) around

8. (F) does

    (G) stopped

    (H) away

    (J) befor

DIRECTIONS: Choose the best answer.

9. **Which word in the following sentence needs to be capitalized?**

    I went to the store with my friend on monday.

    (A) Store

    (B) My

    (C) Friend

    (D) Monday

10. **Which punctuation mark is missing from the following sentence?**

    Why isn't Skye happy today

    (F) .

    (G) ?

    (H) !

    (J) none

DIRECTIONS: Read each choice. Choose the answer that makes a complete, correct sentence.

11. **Li helped _____ .**

    (A) around the house

    (B) wants lots of sunny days

    (C) with many friends

    (D) played basketball

12. **_____ to get on the plane.**

    (F) You need a ticket

    (G) Some people

    (H) Wearing a seat belt

    (J) This corner

13. **Jamal's dog _____ .**

    (A) my shoes

    (B) was licking his paws

    (C) running toward

    (D) she said

14. **_____ a sand castle at the beach.**

    (F) Alicia and her friend

    (G) Alicia wants to play

    (H) Alicia made

    (J) Alicia went

STOP

English Language Arts

7.0

Generating Questions

Research

DIRECTIONS: Read the passages. Then, answer the questions.

Therapy Dogs

Dogs can help people get better after they've been sick. These special dogs are called *therapy dogs.*

The dogs' owners bring them into hospital rooms. They let people meet the dogs. Sometimes, the dogs go right up to the beds. People can pet the dogs, brush them, and talk to them. Studies have shown that being with dogs and other animals can help people heal faster.

Not every dog is a good choice for this important job. A therapy dog must be calm and friendly. Some therapy dog owners feel that their pets were born to help sick people get well again.

1. **Which of the following best summarizes the main point of this story?**

   (A) Therapy dogs like to be brushed.

   (B) Therapy dogs are calm and friendly.

   (C) Therapy dogs help people get better after they've been sick.

   (D) Therapy dogs like to visit hospitals.

2. **What else would you like to know about therapy dogs? On the lines below, write two questions you have about therapy dogs.**

   _____

   _____

   _____

   _____

   _____

   _____

Jellyfish

Jellyfish come in all sizes and colors. Some are only one inch across. Other jellyfish are five feet wide. Some are orange. Others are red. Some jellyfish have no color at all. Gently poke one type of jellyfish with a stick, and it will glow. However, do not let any jellyfish touch you, because they can sting!

3. **Which of the following best summarizes the main point of this story?**

   (F) Jellyfish can sting.

   (G) There are many kinds of jellyfish.

   (H) Some jellyfish are orange.

   (J) Jellyfish can hide.

4. **What else would you like to know about jellyfish? On the lines below, write two questions you have about jellyfish.**

   _____

   _____

   _____

   _____

   _____

   _____

   _____

STOP

English Language Arts

| 8.0 |

Using a Table of Contents and an Index

Research

DIRECTIONS: Read the table of contents and index from a book about art. Then, answer questions 1–3.

```
TABLE OF CONTENTS

Painting . . . . . . . . . . . . . . . . . . . . . . . . 3
Drawing . . . . . . . . . . . . . . . . . . . . . . . 14
Index . . . . . . . . . . . . . . . . . . . . . . . . . 53
Glossary . . . . . . . . . . . . . . . . . . . . . . . 57
```

```
INDEX

colors . . . . . . . . . . . . . . . . . . . . 8, 22, 31
museums . . . . . . . . . . . . . . . 2,10,19, 35
pencil . . . . . . . . . . . . . . . . . . . . . . . . . 16
watercolor paints . . . . . . . . . . . . . . . . . 5
```

1. **Which page does the chapter about drawing start on?**
    - Ⓐ page 3
    - Ⓑ page 14
    - Ⓒ page 53
    - Ⓓ page 57

2. **If you wanted to find the glossary, which page would you turn to?**
    - Ⓕ page 3
    - Ⓖ page 14
    - Ⓗ page 53
    - Ⓙ page 57

3. **Which pages would you look at to find out about museums?**
    - Ⓐ pages 8, 22, and 31
    - Ⓑ pages 2, 10, 19, and 35
    - Ⓒ page 14
    - Ⓓ page 29

DIRECTIONS: Read the table of contents and index from a book about some states in the U.S. Then, answer questions 4–6.

```
TABLE OF CONTENTS

Alabama . . . . . . . . . . . . . . . . . . . . . . . 2
Alaska . . . . . . . . . . . . . . . . . . . . . . . 12
Arizona . . . . . . . . . . . . . . . . . . . . . . . 25
Index . . . . . . . . . . . . . . . . . . . . . . . . 36
```

```
INDEX

education . . . . . . . . . . . . . . . 7,15,19, 27
industry . . . . . . . . . . . . . . . . . . . . . 5, 23
population . . . . . . . . . . . . . . 4,17, 26, 32
resources . . . . . . . . . . . . . . . . . 6,13, 25
```

4. **If you were doing a report on Alaska, which pages would you turn to?**
    - Ⓕ pages 12–24
    - Ⓖ pages 34–45
    - Ⓗ pages 46–54
    - Ⓙ pages 2–11

5. **The chapter on Arizona starts on page _____ .**
    - Ⓐ 2
    - Ⓒ 25
    - Ⓑ 12
    - Ⓓ 36

6. **Which pages would you look at to find out about resources in these states?**
    - Ⓕ page 34
    - Ⓖ pages 6, 13, and 25
    - Ⓗ pages 5 and 23
    - Ⓙ pages 11, 29, and 46

STOP

English Language Arts

8.0

Using a Dictionary

Research

***

DIRECTIONS: Read the questions carefully. Choose the correct answers.

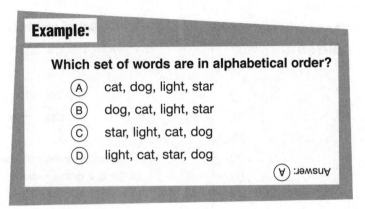

Example:

Which set of words are in alphabetical order?

(A) cat, dog, light, star

(B) dog, cat, light, star

(C) star, light, cat, dog

(D) light, cat, star, dog

Answer: (A)

Clue

When you are alphabetizing, look at the next letter in the word if the first letters are the same.

1. **The guide words at the top of your dictionary page are *face—fish*. Which word will you find on the page?**

   (A) full

   (B) time

   (C) enough

   (D) factory

2. **In the dictionary, which word comes after *hot dog*?**

   (F) egg

   (G) cat food

   (H) ham

   (J) milk

3. **Which set of words is in alphabetical order?**

   (A) bike, bus, came, done

   (B) bus, bike, done, came

   (C) came, done, bus, bike

   (D) bike, came, bus, done

4. **Which guide words should you look for if you are looking for the word *mountain*?**

   (F) math—mask

   (G) mother—mouth

   (H) math—meat

   (J) mystery—myth

5. **Which set of words is not in alphabetical order?**

   (A) day, deep, fly

   (B) keep, just, line

   (C) heavy, inside, kite

   (D) reason, sick, today

6. **In the dictionary, which word comes before *pants*?**

   (F) soccer ball

   (G) puppy

   (H) snake

   (J) football

STOP

English Language Arts

| 7.0–8.0 |

For pages 41–43

| **Mini-Test 3** |

Research

DIRECTIONS: Use the table of contents below to answer questions 1–3.

```
┌─────────────────────────────────────┐
│       TABLE OF CONTENTS              │
│                                      │
│  Introduction . . . . . . . . . . 1  │
│  Butterflies . . . . . . . . . . . 2 │
│  Bees . . . . . . . . . . . . . . 16 │
│  Spiders . . . . . . . . . . . . 25  │
│  Ants . . . . . . . . . . . . . . 39 │
│  Index . . . . . . . . . . . . . 53  │
│  Glossary . . . . . . . . . . . . 57 │
└─────────────────────────────────────┘
```

1. **Which pages would you look at to read about butterflies?**

   (A) pages 2–15

   (B) pages 16–24

   (C) pages 25–38

   (D) pages 39–52

2. **Where can Max find out which pages have information about spider webs?**

   (F) under *Ants* on page 39

   (G) in the glossary

   (H) in the index

   (J) in the introduction

3. **Where can Sue find information about bees?**

   (A) pages 2–15

   (B) pages 16–24

   (C) pages 25–38

   (D) pages 39–52

DIRECTIONS: Choose the correct answer.

4. **Which set of words is in alphabetical order?**

   (F) bakery, art, pet, bookstore

   (G) art, bakery, bookstore, pet

   (H) art, bookstore, bakery, pet

   (J) art, pet, bakery, bookstore

5. **The guide words at the top of a dictionary page are *good—green*. Which word could you find on the page?**

   (A) girl

   (B) game

   (C) had

   (D) great

6. **If you put this list of names in alphabetical order, who will be before *Makayla*?**

   (F) Isabella

   (G) Mark

   (H) Nathan

   (J) Scott

7. **Which set of words is in alphabetical order?**

   (A) bench, swing, duck, path

   (B) bench, duck, swing, path

   (C) duck, bench, path, swing

   (D) bench, duck, path, swing

STOP

English Language Arts

| 9.0 |

Understanding Language Use

Cultural and Social Language Use

DIRECTIONS: Read the paragraphs about how people talk in the country of India. India is a country near China. Then, answer the questions.

India

In the United States, most people speak English. In India, there are more than 1,000 different languages. This has caused many problems. Many of the people speak the words in different ways. Hindi was chosen as the main way to speak to solve the problem. However, it is still hard for people to talk to each other.

There are many ways to let others know what you think without using words. Some actions mean different things in India. For example, to show an older person that you respect him, bow down and touch his feet. If you want to be rude, sit with the bottoms of your shoes showing. To show you are clean, never wear your shoes in the house or in the kitchen. If you don't want to be polite, point at your feet.

1. **What is the main idea of the passage?**

   (A) It is fun to live in India.

   (B) Learning to read is important.

   (C) Never point at your feet or show the bottom of your shoes.

   (D) In India, there are many ways to let others know what you think without words.

2. **Based on the passage, what is rude in India?**

   (F) never wearing your shoes in the house

   (G) learning how to read

   (H) sitting with the bottoms of your shoes showing

   (J) going to the store

3. **Based on the passage, what can you do to show respect in India?**

   (A) wear your socks outside

   (B) bow down and touch an older person's feet

   (C) frown at people

   (D) talk quietly

4. **What are you showing by not wearing your shoes in the house?**

   (F) You are rude.

   (G) Your feet smell.

   (H) You are clean.

   (J) You are polite.

STOP

Name _____ Date _____

English Language Arts

Sharing a Response to Reading
Cultural and Social Language Use

DIRECTIONS: Think about your class at school as being a small community. In your class, you get to read books with other students. Sometimes, your class will read and discuss a book together. Think about the last book that was read to your class. In the box below, draw a picture about something you or your class did or did not like about the book. Write a couple of sentences to explain your picture. Then, share your page with another student in your class. Did you pick the same or different things to write about the book?

_____
_____
_____
_____
_____
_____
_____
_____
_____

STOP

English Language Arts

| 12.0 |

Sharing a
Book Review
Cultural and Social Language Use

DIRECTIONS: Think of a book that you read by yourself that you really liked. Write a review of your favorite book by answering the questions below. Try not to give away the ending so your friends can enjoy the story, too!

1. The title of my favorite book is

_____

_____

_____

_____ .

2. Look at the following list. Put a check mark in any of the boxes that describe your book. This book has:

❑   a funny story.

❑   a sad story.

❑   a surprise ending.

❑   interesting characters.

❑   a lot of facts.

❑   poems.

❑   nice pictures.

❑   comic strips.

3. This book is about

_____

_____

_____

_____

_____

_____

_____

_____

_____

_____

_____ .

4. I would tell my friends to read this book because

_____

_____

_____

_____

_____

_____

_____

_____

_____

_____

_____

_____ .

5. Share your book review with a friend or with your class.

STOP

English Language Arts

| 9.0–12.0 |

For pages 45–47

Mini-Test 4

Cultural and Social Language Use

DIRECTIONS: Read the story. Then, answer the questions.

Japan

In Japan, people show respect to one another in different ways. Men and women bow to show respect to each other. They also bow when they say *hello* or *thank you.* When bowing, they keep their feet together and their backs straight.

It is rude to point at others or chew gum while talking in Japan. Women are also taught to place their hand in front of their mouth when they laugh. They do this so their teeth do not show.

Japanese schools are very strict. Students must show respect to their teachers. One way they might do this is to bow to their teachers at the beginning and end of each class. Showing respect is an important part of life in Japan.

1. **What is the main idea of this passage?**

    (A) It is rude to point at others while talking.

    (B) Japan is fun to visit.

    (C) Japanese schools are very strict.

    (D) The Japanese show respect to one another in different ways.

2. **Based on the passage, what is rude in Japan?**

    (F) bowing when saying thank you

    (G) chewing gum while talking

    (H) wearing a uniform to school

    (J) bowing to a teacher

3. **Based on the passage, what can you do to show respect in Japan?**

    (A) wave to say *hello*

    (B) bow to say *thank you*

    (C) snap your gum while talking

    (D) point at others while talking

4. **Why is it important to read about how people talk and act in other countries?**

    (F) to learn that people have different ways of talking and acting

    (G) to find out how students act in other countries

    (H) to learn about good manners

    (J) to learn that people talk and act the same way in every country

STOP

How Am I Doing?

Mini-Test 1

Page 22

Number Correct

11–13 answers correct	**Great Job!** Move on to the section test on page 51.
6–10 answers correct	**You're almost there!** But you still need a little practice. Review practice pages 7–21 before moving on to the section test on page 51.
0–5 answers correct	**Oops!** Time to review what you have learned and try again. Review the practice section on pages 7–21. Then, retake the test on page 22. Now, move on to the section test on page 51.

Mini-Test 2

Page 39

Number Correct

11–14 answers correct	**Awesome!** Move on to the section test on page 51.
6–10 answers correct	**You're almost there!** But you still need a little practice. Review practice pages 24–38 before moving on to the section test on page 51.
0–5 answers correct	**Oops!** Time to review what you have learned and try again. Review the practice section on pages 24–38. Then, retake the test on page 39. Now, move on to the section test on page 51.

Mini-Test 3

Page 44

Number Correct

6–7 answers correct	**Great Job!** Move on to the section test on page 51.
4–5 answers correct	**You're almost there!** But you still need a little practice. Review practice pages 41–43 before moving on to the section test on page 51.
0–3 answers correct	**Oops!** Time to review what you have learned and try again. Review the practice section on pages 41–43. Then, retake the test on page 44. Now, move on to the section test on page 51.

How Am I Doing?

Mini-Test 4	4 answers correct	**Great Job!** Move on to the section test on page 51.
Page 48 **Number Correct**	3 answers correct	**You're almost there!** But you still need a little practice. Review practice pages 45–47 before moving on to the section test on page 51.
	0–2 answers correct	**Oops!** Time to review what you have learned and try again. Review the practice section on pages 45–47. Then, retake the test on page 48. Now, move on to the section test on page 51.

Final English Language Arts Test
for pages 7–48

DIRECTIONS: Read the story. Then, answer questions 1–5.

Cassie's mom has errands to run. Cassie agrees to babysit her little brother. He's sleeping in his room. Her mom leaves Cassie a list of chores to do while she is gone. But when her mom gets back, Cassie will be able to go to the mall with her friends if her chores are done.

As soon as her mom leaves, Cassie starts calling her friends. She talks to Kim for 20 minutes. Then, she talks to Beth for 30 minutes. She calls Jackie after that.

After talking on the phone, Cassie paints her nails while she watches a TV show. Then, she listens to the radio and reads a book. Before Cassie knows it, three hours have passed. Her mom is back home.

Her mom walks in the door. She finds that the kitchen is still a mess. There are crumbs all over the carpet and Cassie's little brother is screaming in his room.

1. Who is the main character in this story?

- (A) Cassie's mom
- (B) Cassie's little brother
- (C) Cassie
- (D) Cassie's friend Kim

2. What is the setting for the story?

- (F) Cassie's school
- (G) Cassie's house
- (H) the mall
- (J) Kim's house

3. This story is which genre or type of writing?

- (A) biography
- (B) nonfiction
- (C) poetry
- (D) fiction

4. Why did the author write this story?

- (F) to give you information
- (G) to get you to believe something
- (H) to entertain you
- (J) to explain how to do something

5. What do you think Cassie's mom did when she got home?

- (A) She was glad that Cassie had fun.
- (B) She thanked Cassie for watching her brother.
- (C) She was unhappy that Cassie had not done her chores.
- (D) She ignored the mess.

DIRECTIONS: Choose the word that best fits in the blanks.

Alicia and her brother Randy hurried out the ___(6)___ in their heavy snowsuits. They played in the snow. They made a big snowman in the ___(7)___ .

6.
- (F) door
- (G) window
- (H) space
- (J) slide

7.
- (A) kitchen
- (B) sand
- (C) garage
- (D) backyard

GO

Name _____ Date _____

DIRECTIONS: Choose the best answer.

8. **Which answer shows what this contraction means?**

   that's

   Ⓕ that is

   Ⓖ that all

   Ⓗ that will

   Ⓙ that calls

9. **Which set of words is in alphabetical order?**

   Ⓐ bat, bend, ant, apple

   Ⓑ bend, bat, ant, apple

   Ⓒ ant, apple, bat, bent

   Ⓓ apple, ant, bat, bend

10. **Where would you look to find information about sharks?**

    Ⓕ in a newspaper

    Ⓖ in an atlas

    Ⓗ in a dictionary

    Ⓙ in an encyclopedia

11. **Where would you look to find a map of the United States?**

    Ⓐ in a newspaper

    Ⓑ in an atlas

    Ⓒ in a dictionary

    Ⓓ in an encyclopedia

12. **Which word has the same ending sound as *block*?**

    Ⓕ box

    Ⓖ breeze

    Ⓗ blue

    Ⓙ think

13. **Which word has the same vowel sound as *stood*?**

    Ⓐ two

    Ⓑ those

    Ⓒ road

    Ⓓ could

DIRECTIONS: Read the table of contents. Then, answer questions 14 and 15.

14. **Which chapter starts on page 85?**

    Ⓕ Zoos of the World

    Ⓖ Creatures of the Sea

    Ⓗ Rodents

    Ⓙ Insects and Spiders

15. **Which page does the chapter titled "Animals Around the World" start on?**

    Ⓐ page 11

    Ⓑ page 59

    Ⓒ page 101

    Ⓓ page 112

DIRECTIONS: Choose the best answer.

16. **Which word is a synonym for *smart*?**

    Ⓕ dull

    Ⓖ secret

    Ⓗ clever

    Ⓙ bored

GO

17. Which word is an antonym for *excited*?

(A) calm

(B) left

(C) dirty

(D) open

DIRECTIONS: Read the sentence. Choose the phrase that best fits in the blank.

18. The train blew its whistle as it _____ .

(F) to go around in circles

(G) passed through town

(H) for very fast tracks

(J) talking to my dad

19. Juan has a bad cold and does not feel _____ .

(A) leaving his socks out

(B) soup is good

(C) like eating dinner

(D) around the house

20. The puppy ran _____ and got all wet.

(F) barks a lot

(G) eats his dog treats

(H) through the sprinkler

(J) treating us to ice cream

DIRECTIONS: Read each choice. Chose the one that is a complete sentence.

21. (A) Basketball with her friends.

(B) The storm was so.

(C) Red and black checkers.

(D) Five children are on the team.

22. (F) Prize for baking the pie.

(G) Today was a great day.

(H) Dirt off your hands.

(J) Jump up and wag its tail.

DIRECTIONS: Read the passage. Answer the questions that follow.

Giraffes are the tallest animals. They have long necks and long legs. They live on the grasslands in Africa. Giraffes live in small groups called *herds.*

A giraffe uses its long tongue to grab leaves from tall tree branches. A giraffe has to spread its front legs apart and lower its head to drink water.

23. Which sentence does not belong in this passage?

(A) It is very hot in Africa.

(B) A giraffe eats mostly leaves.

(C) A giraffe's tongue is about 24 inches long.

(D) A giraffe can grow to be 18 feet tall.

24. Which sentence belongs in this passage?

(F) My friend Kendal has a stuffed giraffe.

(G) I can spell the word *giraffe.*

(H) A giraffe can go weeks without water if it has to.

(J) Tanya wants to go to Africa one day.

DIRECTIONS: Choose the word that is not spelled correctly.

25. (A) until

(B) numbr

(C) happy

(D) family

26. (F) everything

(G) doesn't

(H) build

(J) haveing

27. (A) terned

(B) throw

(C) corner

(D) while

Final English Language Arts Test

Answer Sheet

1. Ⓐ Ⓑ Ⓒ Ⓓ
2. Ⓕ Ⓖ Ⓗ Ⓙ
3. Ⓐ Ⓑ Ⓒ Ⓓ
4. Ⓕ Ⓖ Ⓗ Ⓙ
5. Ⓐ Ⓑ Ⓒ Ⓓ
6. Ⓕ Ⓖ Ⓗ Ⓙ
7. Ⓐ Ⓑ Ⓒ Ⓓ
8. Ⓕ Ⓖ Ⓗ Ⓙ
9. Ⓐ Ⓑ Ⓒ Ⓓ
10. Ⓕ Ⓖ Ⓗ Ⓙ

11. Ⓐ Ⓑ Ⓒ Ⓓ
12. Ⓕ Ⓖ Ⓗ Ⓙ
13. Ⓐ Ⓑ Ⓒ Ⓓ
14. Ⓕ Ⓖ Ⓗ Ⓙ
15. Ⓐ Ⓑ Ⓒ Ⓓ
16. Ⓕ Ⓖ Ⓗ Ⓙ
17. Ⓐ Ⓑ Ⓒ Ⓓ
18. Ⓕ Ⓖ Ⓗ Ⓙ
19. Ⓐ Ⓑ Ⓒ Ⓓ
20. Ⓕ Ⓖ Ⓗ Ⓙ

21. Ⓐ Ⓑ Ⓒ Ⓓ
22. Ⓕ Ⓖ Ⓗ Ⓙ
23. Ⓐ Ⓑ Ⓒ Ⓓ
24. Ⓕ Ⓖ Ⓗ Ⓙ
25. Ⓐ Ⓑ Ⓒ Ⓓ
26. Ⓕ Ⓖ Ⓗ Ⓙ
27. Ⓐ Ⓑ Ⓒ Ⓓ

Mathematics Standards

Standard 1—Number and Operations *(See pages 57–67.)*
  A. Understand numbers, ways of representing numbers, relationships among numbers, and number systems.
  B. Understand meanings of operations and how they relate to one another.
  C. Compute fluently and make reasonable estimates.

Standard 2—Algebra *(See pages 68–73.)*
  A. Understand patterns, relations, and functions.
  B. Represent and analyze mathematical situations and structures using algebraic symbols.
  C. Use mathematical models to represent and understand quantitative relationships.
  D. Analyze change in various contexts.

What it means:
- Students should be able to model whole-number addition and subtraction situations using objects, pictures, and symbols.

Standard 3—Geometry *(See pages 76–82.)*
  A. Analyze characteristics and properties of two- and three-dimensional shapes and develop mathematical arguments about geometric relationships.
  B. Specify locations and describe spatial relationships using coordinate geometry and other representational systems.
  C. Apply transformations and use symmetry to analyze mathematical situations.
  D. Use visualization, spatial reasoning, and geometric modeling to solve problems.

What it means:
- Students should be able to recognize transformations such as slides, flips, and turns, and identify shapes that have symmetry.

Standard 4—Measurement *(See pages 83–86.)*
  A. Understand measurable attributes of objects and the units, systems, and processes of measurement.
  B. Apply appropriate techniques, tools, and formulas to determine measurement.

What it means:
- Students should be able to measure length, volume, weight, area, and time, selecting appropriate units for what is being measured. Practicing with nonstandard as well as standard units will help students learn to apply appropriate measurement techniques.

Mathematics Standards

Standard 5—Data Analysis and Probability *(See pages 89–92.)*

A. Formulate questions that can be addressed with data and collect, organize, and display relevant data to answer them.

B. Select and use appropriate statistical methods to analyze data.

C. Develop and evaluate inferences and predictions that are based on data.

D. Understand and apply basic concepts of probability.

What it means:

- Students should be able to analyze data represented in simple graphs.
- Students should be able to determine the outcomes of events as likely or unlikely.

Standard 6—Process *(See pages 93–97.)*

A. Problem Solving

B. Reasoning and Proof

C. Communication

D. Connections

E. Representation

Name _____ Date _____

Mathematics

Understanding Numbers

Number and Operations

DIRECTIONS: Choose the best answer.

1. **Which number matches the base 10 blocks?**

   (A) 43
   (B) 68
   (C) 51
   (D) 57

   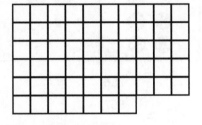

2. **Which squares contain numbers that are all less than 19?**

   (F) 7 15 10 18
   (G) 91 20 32 57
   (H) 18 6 23 65
   (J) 12 81 17 44

3. **Which numbers should go in the blank spaces when you count by ones?**

   | 38, 39, _____, 41, 42, 43, _____ |

   (A) 40 and 44
   (B) 29 and 45
   (C) 30 and 46
   (D) 39 and 44

4. **Which number is the expanded numeral for seven hundred eighty-six?**

   (F) 60 + 80 + 70
   (G) 70 + 80 + 60
   (H) 700 + 80 + 6
   (J) 70 + 86

5. **Which numeral means seven hundreds, three tens, and five ones?**

   (A) 735
   (B) 7035
   (C) 7305
   (D) 739

6. **Which number matches the word in the box?**

   | **five hundred thirty six** |

   (F) 5,306
   (G) 356
   (H) 5,036
   (J) 536

7. **If you are counting by ones, which number word should go in the box?**

   | **twenty-nine, _____ , thirty-one, thirty-two** |

   (A) thirty
   (B) forty
   (C) fifty
   (D) twenty-eight

GO

8. Which group of numbers is in the correct counting order?

   (F) 79, 78, 77, 80, 81

   (G) 78, 79, 77, 80, 81

   (H) 77, 78, 79, 80, 81

   (J) 79, 77, 78, 81, 80

9. Look at the flowers. Which group of base 10 blocks has the same number as the flowers?

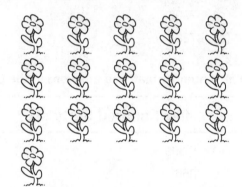

(A)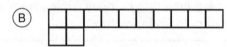

(B)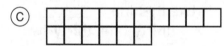

(C)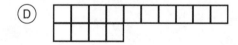

(D)

10. Look at the hundreds, tens, and ones chart. Which number is represented by the dots on the chart?

100s	10s	1s

   (F) 756

   (G) 857

   (H) 847

   (J) 846

11. Which word stands for the number in the box?

43

   (A) thirty-four

   (B) forty

   (C) forty-three

   (D) forty-four

12. Which number matches the number in the middle of the box?

11, 12, 13, 14, 15

   (F) eleven

   (G) thirteen

   (H) fifteen

   (J) twelve

STOP

Mathematics

[1.A]

Identifying Place Values

Number and Operations

DIRECTIONS: Choose the best answer.

1. **Which digit is in the hundreds place?**

   | 401 |

   (A) 4
   (B) 0
   (C) 1
   (D) none of the above

2. **What is the place value of number 8?**

   | 582 |

   (F) ones
   (G) tens
   (H) hundreds
   (J) thousands

DIRECTIONS: Use the following set of numbers to answer questions 3 and 4.

791, 792, 793, 794, 795

3. **What is the place value of the 7s?**

   (A) ones
   (B) tens
   (C) hundreds
   (D) thousands

4. **What is the place value of the 9s?**

   (F) ones
   (G) tens
   (H) hundreds
   (J) thousands

DIRECTIONS: Choose the best answer.

5. **Which digit is in the hundreds place?**

   | 4016 |

   (A) 4
   (B) 0
   (C) 1
   (D) 6

6. **What is the place value of the number 5?**

   | 945 |

   (F) ones
   (G) tens
   (H) hundreds
   (J) thousands

7. **Which number has 6 ones and 3 hundreds?**

   (A) 563
   (B) 653
   (C) 356
   (D) 536

8. **Which number has 4 hundreds, 5 tens, and 2 ones?**

   (F) 524
   (G) 542
   (H) 425
   (J) 452

STOP

Name _____ Date _____

Mathematics

 1.A

Naming Fractional Parts

Number and Operations

DIRECTIONS: Choose the best answer.

1. Which shape is one-third shaded?

2. How much of the figure below is shaded?

(F) $\frac{2}{3}$

(G) $\frac{4}{8}$

(H) $\frac{2}{6}$

(J) $\frac{4}{6}$

3. How much of the circle below is shaded?

(A) $\frac{5}{6}$

(B) $\frac{4}{6}$

(C) $\frac{1}{2}$

(D) $\frac{1}{6}$

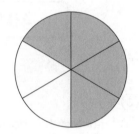

4. Which of these figures shows $\frac{3}{4}$?

(F)

(G)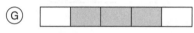

(H)

(J)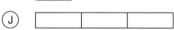

DIRECTIONS: Express the shaded parts as a fraction. The first one has been done for you.

5.

$\frac{4}{5}$

6.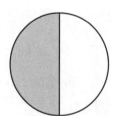

_____

7.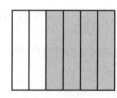

_____

8.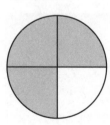

_____

9.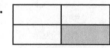

_____

10.

_____

STOP

Mathematics 1.A

60

Spectrum Test Prep Grade 2

Name _____   Date _____

Mathematics

| 1.B |

Understanding Operations

Number and Operations

DIRECTIONS: Read each question. Then, choose the best answer.

1. **How many problems have an answer equal to four?**

7	8	9	2	1
+ 3	− 4	− 6	+ 2	+ 3

- Ⓐ 4
- Ⓑ 1
- Ⓒ 5
- Ⓓ 3

2. **Which multiplication fact is shown by the dots?**

- Ⓕ 3 × 4 = 12
- Ⓖ 3 × 6 = 18
- Ⓗ 4 × 4 = 16
- Ⓙ 2 × 9 = 18

3. **Which group of number statements equals the same as the word in the box?**

> ## eight

- Ⓐ 10 − 5
       3 + 2
- Ⓑ 4 + 4
       11 − 3
- Ⓒ 13 − 6
       4 + 3
- Ⓓ 8 + 3
       15 − 4

4. **Five ants live together. Four ants go out for a walk. Which number sentence shows how many ants stay home?**

- Ⓕ 5 − 4 = 1
- Ⓖ 5 + 4 = 9
- Ⓗ 9 − 5 = 4
- Ⓙ 6 + 4 = 10

5. **Look at the number sentence in the box. Which number is the best estimate for your answer?**

> ## 276 + 88 = ☐

- Ⓐ 100
- Ⓑ 600
- Ⓒ 200
- Ⓓ 400

STOP

Mathematics

1.B

Relating Addition and Subtraction

Number and Operations

DIRECTIONS: Find the missing number that solves both number sentences.

Example:

$$11 - \boxed{6} = 5$$

$$5 + \boxed{6} = 11$$

The number that solves both number sentences is 6.

 Clue   Try each answer choice in both boxes. Find one choice that makes both sentences true.

1. $7 + \square = 15$
    $15 - \square = 7$
    - (A) 8
    - (B) 7
    - (C) 9
    - (D) 5

2. $25 - \square = 20$
   $20 + \square = 25$
    - (F) 7
    - (G) 6
    - (H) 5
    - (J) 4

3. $3 + \square = 13$
    $13 - \square = 3$
    - (A) 9
    - (B) 10
    - (C) 11
    - (D) 8

4. $14 - \square = 6$
   $6 + \square = 14$
    - (F) 9
    - (G) 8
    - (H) 6
    - (J) 7

5. $5 + 7 = \square$
   $\square - 5 = 7$
    - (A) 11
    - (B) 13
    - (C) 12
    - (D) 14

6. $10 - 6 = \square$
   $\square + 6 = 10$
    - (F) 3
    - (G) 4
    - (H) 5
    - (J) 6

STOP

Name _____ Date _____

| 1.B |

Modeling Multiplication

Number and Operations

DIRECTIONS: Use multiplication to find the answers.

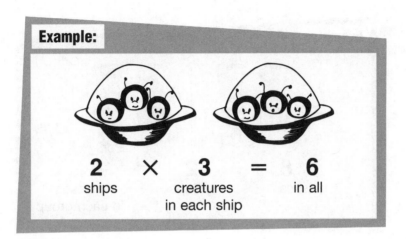

Example:

| **2** | × | **3** | = | **6** |
| ships | | creatures in each ship | | in all |

1. $3 \times 4 =$ _____

4. $2 \times 5 =$ _____

2. $5 \times 1 =$ _____

5. $3 \times 3 =$ _____

3. $7 \times 2 =$ _____

6. $4 \times 2 =$ _____

STOP

Mathematics

1.B

Modeling Division

Number and Operations

DIRECTIONS: Use division to find the answers.

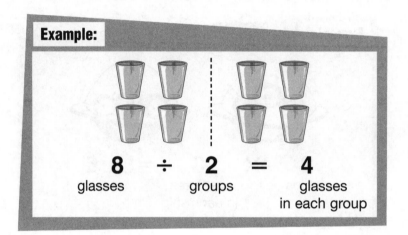

Example:

8 ÷ **2** = **4**

glasses   groups   glasses in each group

1. $12 \div 3 =$ _____

4. $8 \div 4 =$ _____

2. $10 \div 2 =$ _____

5. $4 \div 2 =$ _____

3. $6 \div 3 =$ _____

6. $9 \div 3 =$ _____

STOP

Mathematics

| 1.C |

Addition

Number and Operations

DIRECTIONS: Solve each addition problem.

1. $\begin{array}{r} 7 \\ + 11 \\ \hline \end{array}$
    - (A) 19
    - (B) 18
    - (C) 16
    - (D) 17

2. $\begin{array}{r} 6 \\ + 2 \\ \hline \end{array}$
    - (F) 5
    - (G) 11
    - (H) 8
    - (J) 4

3. $\begin{array}{r} 2 \\ + 8 \\ \hline \end{array}$
    - (A) 10
    - (B) 6
    - (C) 28
    - (D) 11

4. $\begin{array}{r} 12 \\ + 3 \\ \hline \end{array}$
    - (F) 16
    - (G) 17
    - (H) 18
    - (J) 15

5. $5 + 5 =$
    - (A) 5
    - (B) 55
    - (C) 10
    - (D) 0

6. $12 + 4 =$
    - (F) 16
    - (G) 14
    - (H) 22
    - (J) 8

7. $9 + 1 + 4 =$
    - (A) 13
    - (B) 5
    - (C) 14
    - (D) 15

8. $6 + 3 + 2 =$
    - (F) 65
    - (G) 12
    - (H) 5
    - (J) 11

9. $\begin{array}{r} 10 \\ 5 \\ + 2 \\ \hline \end{array}$
    - (A) 107
    - (B) 7
    - (C) 17
    - (D) 3

10. $5 + 11 =$
    - (F) 16
    - (G) 17
    - (H) 6
    - (J) 15

11. $\begin{array}{r} 3 \\ 8 \\ + 5 \\ \hline \end{array}$
    - (A) 16
    - (B) 10
    - (C) 2
    - (D) 21

12. $\begin{array}{r} 4 \\ 7 \\ + 1 \\ \hline \end{array}$
    - (F) 10
    - (G) 13
    - (H) 2
    - (J) 12

STOP

Mathematics

1.C

Subtraction

Number and Operations

DIRECTIONS: Solve each subtraction problem.

1. 49
    − 23

    Ⓐ 52
    Ⓑ 26
    Ⓒ 36
    Ⓓ 62

2. 26 − 5 =

    Ⓕ 21
    Ⓖ 11
    Ⓗ 9
    Ⓙ 22

3. 95 − 78 =

    Ⓐ 17
    Ⓑ 27
    Ⓒ 23
    Ⓓ 13

4. 66 − 49 =

    Ⓕ 27
    Ⓖ 17
    Ⓗ 19
    Ⓙ 18

5. 83
    − 74

    Ⓐ 11
    Ⓑ 14
    Ⓒ 19
    Ⓓ 9

6. 68
    − 21

    Ⓕ 57
    Ⓖ 47
    Ⓗ 48
    Ⓙ 49

7. 17 − 14 =

    Ⓐ 2
    Ⓑ 3
    Ⓒ 4
    Ⓓ 5

8. 86
    − 8

    Ⓕ 76
    Ⓖ 89
    Ⓗ 82
    Ⓙ 78

9. 36 − 7 =

    Ⓐ 19
    Ⓑ 31
    Ⓒ 30
    Ⓓ 29

10. 92
     − 56

    Ⓕ 46
    Ⓖ 45
    Ⓗ 36
    Ⓙ 34

11. 49 − 11 =

    Ⓐ 60
    Ⓑ 38
    Ⓒ 37
    Ⓓ 29

12. 35
     − 12

    Ⓕ 27
    Ⓖ 33
    Ⓗ 47
    Ⓙ 23

STOP

Mathematics

| 1.C |

Solving Addition and Subtraction Problems
Number and Operations

DIRECTIONS: Choose the best answer.

1. **Twenty students are in a lunch line. Emma is thirteenth in line. Which number sentence shows how many students are behind Emma?**

   (A) $20 + 13 = 33$

   (B) $33 - 13 = 20$

   (C) $20 - 13 = 7$

   (D) $20 + 7 = 27$

2. **Thirty-nine ants live in the ant farm. Twenty-seven leave the farm. Which number sentence shows how many ants are left in the ant farm?**

   (F) $39 - 27 = 12$

   (G) $39 + 27 = 66$

   (H) $66 - 27 = 39$

   (J) $12 + 39 = 51$

3. **A single-scoop ice-cream cone used to cost 79 cents. The price has gone up 19 cents. How much does it cost now?**

   (A) 89¢

   (B) 78¢

   (C) 98¢

   (D) 99¢

4. **Notebooks at the school store cost 60 cents each, and pens cost 35 cents. If Hayden wants to buy one pen and one notebook, how much money will he need?**

   (F) 90¢

   (G) 95¢

   (H) 85¢

   (J) 25¢

5. **Jenna's grandpa is 78 years old and her grandma is 73 years old. How many years are their ages together?**

   (A) 150

   (B) 141

   (C) 148

   (D) 151

6. **Carter and Max were having a football-throwing contest. Carter threw it 62 feet and Max threw it 48 feet. How much farther did Carter throw the ball than Max?**

   (F) 4 feet

   (G) 7 feet

   (H) 12 feet

   (J) 14 feet

7. **Latisha's mom baked 76 cookies yesterday. Latisha took 24 cookies to her class at school. Which number sentence shows how many cookies were left at home?**

   (A) $76 + 24 = 100$

   (B) $100 - 76 = 24$

   (C) $76 - 24 = 52$

   (D) $52 + 24 = 76$

8. **Kara practiced the piano for 36 minutes on Monday, 24 minutes on Wednesday, and 31 minutes on Thursday. How many minutes did she practice in all?**

   (F) 60 minutes

   (G) 81 minutes

   (H) 97 minutes

   (J) 91 minutes

STOP

Mathematics

Identifying and Extending Number Patterns

Algebra

DIRECTIONS: Choose the best answer.

1. **What is the next number after 3, 6, 9, 12?**
   - (A) 13
   - (B) 11
   - (C) 15
   - (D) 14

2. **What is the next number after 4, 8, 12, 16?**
   - (F) 14
   - (G) 20
   - (H) 15
   - (J) 16

3. **What is the next number after 10, 12, 14, 16?**
   - (A) 17
   - (B) 18
   - (C) 19
   - (D) 20

4. **What is the next number after 10, 15, 20, 25?**
   - (F) 35
   - (G) 36
   - (H) 40
   - (J) 30

5. **What are the next two numbers in this set?**

   20, 30, 40, 50, _____, _____
   - (A) 70, 80
   - (B) 60, 80
   - (C) 60, 70
   - (D) 70, 60

6. **How are these two sets of numbers similar?**

   6, 8, 10, 12
   7, 9, 11, 13
   - (F) both go up by 2
   - (G) both go up by 3
   - (H) both go up by 4
   - (J) both go up by 5

7. **How are these two sets of numbers similar?**

   11, 22, 33, 44
   9, 20, 31, 42
   - (A) both go up by 9
   - (B) both go up by 10
   - (C) both go up by 11
   - (D) both go up by 12

8. **How are these two sets of numbers similar?**

   5, 10, 15, 20
   30, 35, 40, 45
   - (F) both go up by 4
   - (G) both go up by 5
   - (H) both go up by 6
   - (J) both go up by 7

9. **How are these two sets of numbers similar?**

   1, 4, 7, 10
   3, 6, 9, 12
   - (A) both go up by 3
   - (B) both go up by 4
   - (C) both go up by 5
   - (D) both go up by 6

STOP

Name _____   Date _____

Mathematics

2.A

Sorting Objects

Algebra

DIRECTIONS: Look at the shapes below. Then, answer the questions.

1. **One way to sort the objects is by their shape. If you were to put all of the circles in a group, how many would you have?**
   - (A) 3
   - (B) 4
   - (C) 5
   - (D) 6

2. **If you were to put all of the squares in a group, how many would you have?**
   - (F) 3
   - (G) 4
   - (H) 5
   - (J) 6

3. **If you were to put all of the triangles in a group, how many would you have?**
   - (A) 4
   - (B) 5
   - (C) 6
   - (D) 7

4. **Another way to sort the objects is by their color or pattern. How many shapes are gray?**
   - (F) 2
   - (G) 3
   - (H) 4
   - (J) 5

5. **How many shapes are striped?**
   - (A) 3
   - (B) 4
   - (C) 5
   - (D) 6

6. **How many shapes are white?**
   - (F) 4
   - (G) 5
   - (H) 6
   - (J) 7

7. **How many shapes are striped circles?**
   - (A) 1
   - (B) 2
   - (C) 3
   - (D) 4

STOP

Mathematics

2.B

Using Related Operations

Algebra

DIRECTIONS: Choose the best answer.

Examples:

When you add numbers together, the order in which you add them does not change the answer. For example:

$$6 + 3 = 3 + 6$$

A **fact family** is a set of math facts that uses the same three numbers. For example, all four of the following math facts make up a fact family:

$$2 + 9 = 11$$
$$9 + 2 = 11$$
$$11 - 9 = 2$$
$$11 - 2 = 9$$

1. $14 + 5 =$
   - (A) $5 + 14$
   - (B) $5 - 14$
   - (C) $14 + 14$
   - (D) $5 + 5$

2. $8 + 3 =$
   - (F) $3 + 3$
   - (G) $8 - 3$
   - (H) $3 + 8$
   - (J) $8 + 8$

3. $9 + 2 =$
   - (A) $2 - 9$
   - (B) $2 + 9$
   - (C) $9 + 9$
   - (D) $2 - 3$

4. $5 + 4 =$
   - (F) $5 - 4$
   - (G) $5 + 5$
   - (H) $4 + 5$
   - (J) $4 + 4$

5. **Which sentence fits with this fact family?**
   $4 + 6 = 10$
   - (A) $10 - 6 = 4$
   - (B) $6 + 6 = 12$
   - (C) $7 - 2 = 5$
   - (D) $10 - 5 = 5$

6. **Which sentence fits with this fact family?**
   $8 + 9 = 17$
   - (F) $9 + 3 = 12$
   - (G) $9 + 8 = 17$
   - (H) $8 - 4 = 4$
   - (J) $7 + 9 = 16$

7. **Which sentence does *not* fit with this fact family?**
   $9 - 4 = 5$
   - (A) $5 + 4 = 9$
   - (B) $4 + 5 = 9$
   - (C) $9 - 7 = 1$
   - (D) $9 - 5 = 4$

STOP

Name _____ Date _____

Using Symbolic Notations

Algebra

DIRECTIONS: Choose the answer that makes the number sentence true.

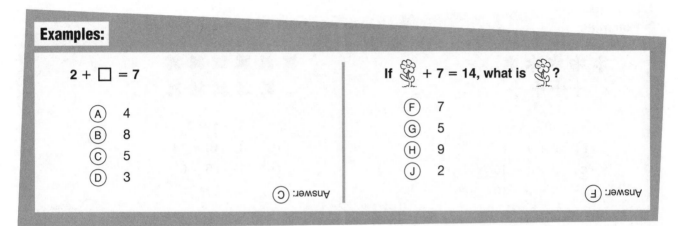

Examples:

$2 + \square = 7$

- Ⓐ 4
- Ⓑ 8
- Ⓒ 5
- Ⓓ 3

Answer: Ⓒ

If 🌼 + 7 = 14, what is 🌼 ?

- Ⓕ 7
- Ⓖ 5
- Ⓗ 9
- Ⓙ 2

Answer: Ⓕ

---

1. $24 - \square = 14$
   - Ⓐ 0
   - Ⓑ 4
   - Ⓒ 10
   - Ⓓ 20

2. $\bigcirc + 7 = 39$
   - Ⓕ 21
   - Ⓖ 32
   - Ⓗ 33
   - Ⓙ 42

3. $35 - \square = 5$
   - Ⓐ 30
   - Ⓑ 20
   - Ⓒ 10
   - Ⓓ 5

4. $\bigcirc - 12 = 12$
   - Ⓕ 10
   - Ⓖ 12
   - Ⓗ 22
   - Ⓙ 24

5. If 🍐 + 16 = 32, what is 🍐 ?
   - Ⓐ 8
   - Ⓑ 21
   - Ⓒ 16
   - Ⓓ 12

6. If 25 + 🐞 = 50, what is 🐞 ?
   - Ⓕ 15
   - Ⓖ 25
   - Ⓗ 30
   - Ⓙ 40

7. If 🤍 + 15 = 25, what is 🤍 ?
   - Ⓐ 40
   - Ⓑ 30
   - Ⓒ 20
   - Ⓓ 10

STOP

Mathematics
2.C

Using Mathematical Models

Algebra

DIRECTIONS: Choose the number sentence that matches the picture.

Examples:

✳ ✳ ✳ ✳ ✳
\+ ✚ ✚ ✚ ✚

(A) $10 - 5 = 5$
(B) $5 + 4 = 9$
(C) $9 + 1 = 10$
(D) $5 + 5 = 10$

Answer: (B)

✖ ✖ ✖ ✖ ✖ ✖
\− ✖ ✖ ✖ ✖ ✖

(F) $3 + 4 = 7$
(G) $4 + 10 = 14$
(H) $12 - 6 = 6$
(J) $6 - 5 = 1$

Answer: (J)

1.

   \+

   (A) $6 + 3 = 9$
   (B) $9 - 3 = 6$
   (C) $3 + 9 = 12$
   (D) $5 - 3 = 8$

2. ⬭⬭⬭⬭⬭⬭⬭

   \+ ▭ ▭ ▭ ▭

   (F) $7 - 4 = 3$
   (G) $11 - 4 = 7$
   (H) $7 + 4 = 11$
   (J) $12 - 9 = 3$

3. ★ ★ ★ ★ ★ ★ ★ ★ ★ ★ ★ ★

   \+ ☆ ☆ ☆ ☆ ☆ ☆ ☆ ☆

   (A) $12 + 12 = 24$
   (B) $21 - 9 = 12$
   (C) $24 - 12 = 12$
   (D) $12 + 9 = 21$

4.

   \−

   (F) $6 - 4 = 2$
   (G) $18 - 7 = 11$
   (H) $6 + 6 = 12$
   (J) $18 - 2 = 16$

5.

   (A) $5 - 3 = 2$
   (B) $5 + 4 = 7$
   (C) $5 - 2 = 3$
   (D) $2 + 5 = 7$

6. ☐☐☐☐☐☐☐☐☐

   \− ☐☐☐☐☐☐☐

   (F) $20 - 11 = 9$
   (G) $11 - 9 = 2$
   (H) $11 + 9 = 20$
   (J) $20 - 9 = 11$

STOP

Mathematics

| 2.D |

Describing Change

Algebra

DIRECTIONS: Read each problem. Choose the best answer that describes each change.

1. Jack and Leo want to split one pizza for lunch. Then they invite a third friend to have some of their pizza, too. What happens to the size of each boy's slice?

   (A) Each slice gets smaller.

   (B) Each slice gets larger.

   (C) The slices stay the same size.

   (D) Each boy gets half of the pizza.

2. LaKeisha is building a tower with blocks. She adds some blocks. Then, she adds more blocks. What happens to the tower?

   (F) The tower does not change.

   (G) The tower gets shorter.

   (H) The tower stays the same size.

   (J) The tower gets taller.

3. Jillian and her sister make a snowman. The sun begins to shine. It gets warmer and warmer. What happens to the snowman?

   (A) The snowman gets bigger.

   (B) The snowman gets smaller.

   (C) The snowman stays the same size.

   (D) Jillian adds a scarf to keep the snowman warm.

4. Kendal's plant is 2 inches tall. Troy's plant is 5 inches tall. Which of these sentences is true?

   (F) Kendal's plant is taller.

   (G) Troy's plant is shorter.

   (H) Kendal's plant is 3 inches shorter than Troy's plant.

   (J) Troy's plant is 3 inches shorter than Kendal's plant.

5. Juanita's softball team scored 4 runs in the first inning, 3 runs in the second inning, and 1 run in the third inning. Which of these sentences is true?

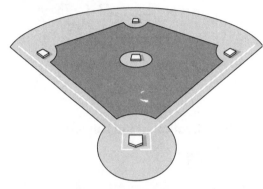

   (A) The number of runs they scored stayed the same each inning.

   (B) The number of runs they scored increased each inning.

   (C) Juanita's team lost the game.

   (D) The number of runs they scored decreased each inning.

6. On Monday, 3 inches of snow fell. On Tuesday, 2 inches of snow fell. On Wednesday, 4 inches of snow fell. Which of these sentences is true?

   (F) The least snow fell on Tuesday.

   (G) The amount of snow stayed the same each day.

   (H) The amount of snow decreased each day.

   (J) The amount of snow increased each day.

STOP

Name _____ Date _____

Mathematics

| 1.A–2.D |

For pages 57–73

Mini-Test 1

Number and Operations; Algebra

DIRECTIONS: Use the picture of the table to answer questions 1–3.

1. **What fraction of the balloons are shaded?**

   Ⓐ $\frac{1}{5}$

   Ⓑ $\frac{2}{5}$

   Ⓒ $\frac{4}{5}$

   Ⓓ $\frac{3}{5}$

2. **What fraction of the plates are shaded?**

   Ⓕ $\frac{3}{6}$

   Ⓖ $\frac{2}{6}$

   Ⓗ $\frac{4}{6}$

   Ⓙ $\frac{1}{6}$

3. **What fraction of the presents are shaded?**

   Ⓐ $\frac{2}{4}$

   Ⓑ $\frac{3}{4}$

   Ⓒ $\frac{2}{3}$

   Ⓓ $\frac{1}{4}$

DIRECTIONS: Choose the best answer.

4. **Which answer shows how many tens and ones are in fifty-seven?**

   Ⓕ 7 tens and 5 ones

   Ⓖ 3 tens and 7 ones

   Ⓗ 5 tens and 4 ones

   Ⓙ 5 tens and 7 ones

5. **Which number matches the word in the box?**

   | nine hundred thirteen |

   Ⓐ 9,013

   Ⓑ 9,413

   Ⓒ 913

   Ⓓ 3,391

6. **Which number means one hundred, five tens, eight ones?**

   Ⓕ 158

   Ⓖ 1,058

   Ⓗ 581

   Ⓙ 5,081

7. **78 + 25 = ☐**

   Ⓐ 23

   Ⓑ 43

   Ⓒ 93

   Ⓓ 103

8. **6 × 2 = ☐**

   Ⓕ 8

   Ⓖ 12

   Ⓗ 10

   Ⓙ 18

GO ▶

9. **Which number matches the base ten blocks?**

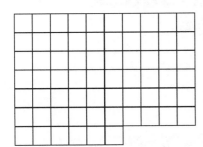

   Ⓐ 45

   Ⓑ 66

   Ⓒ 74

   Ⓓ 76

10. **Which number makes both number sentences true?**

   $9 + \square = 16$

   $16 - \square = 9$

   Ⓕ 7

   Ⓖ 16

   Ⓗ 9

   Ⓙ 10

11.   **85**
   − 37

   Ⓐ 58

   Ⓑ 48

   Ⓒ 47

   Ⓓ 92

12. **Olivia's mom baked 70 cookies for her school party. Olivia brought 48 of them to school. Which number sentence shows the number of cookies left at home?**

   Ⓕ $70 + 48 = 118$

   Ⓖ $118 - 48 = 70$

   Ⓗ $70 - 48 = 22$

   Ⓙ $48 - 12 = 36$

13. **Which number is next in this pattern?**

   14, 18, 22, 26, 30, _____

   Ⓐ 32

   Ⓑ 33

   Ⓒ 34

   Ⓓ 35

14. **$87 + 42 =$**

   Ⓕ $129 - 42$

   Ⓖ $42 + 87$

   Ⓗ $42 - 87$

   Ⓙ $87 + 129$

15. **If $21 + \text{☆} = 42$, what is ☆?**

   Ⓐ 21

   Ⓑ 22

   Ⓒ 23

   Ⓓ 25

16. **Jackie was 45 inches tall in January. In October, she was 49 inches tall. Which of these sentences is true?**

   Ⓕ Jackie was taller in January.

   Ⓖ Jackie was thinner in January.

   Ⓗ Jackie was shorter in October.

   Ⓙ Jackie was taller in October.

STOP

Mathematics

| 3.A |

Identifying Attributes of Shapes
Geometry

DIRECTIONS: Choose the best answer.

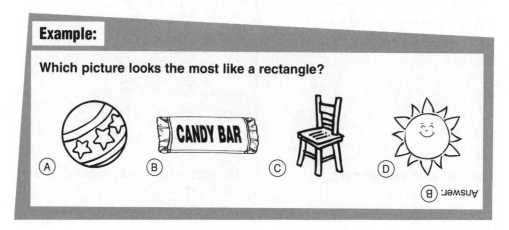

Example:

Which picture looks the most like a rectangle?

(A) (B) CANDY BAR (C) (D)

Answer: (B)

1. **Which figure has three angles or corners?**

   (A) square
   (B) rectangle
   (C) triangle
   (D) circle

2. **How many sides does a rectangle have?**

   (F) 3
   (G) 4
   (H) 5
   (J) 6

3. **What is the name of this figure?**

   (A) sphere
   (B) cone
   (C) cylinder
   (D) cube

4. **A basketball is shaped like a _____ .**

   (F) pyramid
   (G) triangle
   (H) sphere
   (J) rectangle

5. **Which shape is a rectangle?**

   (A) ▱
   (B) ☐
   (C) ▱
   (D) ▭

6. **A shape with 5 sides is known as what?**

   (F) a rectangle
   (G) a square
   (H) a pentagon
   (J) a circle

GO

7. How many of these shapes are cubes?

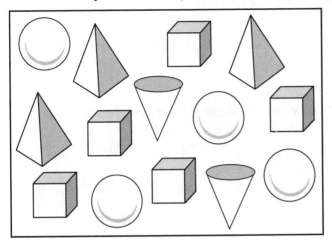

- (A) 2
- (B) 3
- (C) 4
- (D) 5

8. What is the name of this figure?

- (F) cylinder
- (G) cube
- (H) sphere
- (J) triangle

DIRECTIONS: Many everyday objects contain these shapes. For each object shown, choose *cone, cylinder, sphere,* or *none of the above.*

9.
- (A) cone
- (B) cylinder
- (C) sphere
- (D) none of the above

10.
- (F) cone
- (G) cylinder
- (H) sphere
- (J) none of the above

11.
- (A) cone
- (B) cylinder
- (C) sphere
- (D) none of the above

12.
- (F) cone
- (G) cylinder
- (H) sphere
- (J) none of the above

13.
- (A) cone
- (B) cylinder
- (C) sphere
- (D) none of the above

14.
- (F) cone
- (G) cylinder
- (H) sphere
- (J) none of the above

STOP

3.A

Comparing Shapes

Geometry

DIRECTIONS: Choose the best answer.

1. **How is a square different from a rectangle?**

   (A)   A square has four equal sides.

   (B)   A square has two equal sides.

   (C)   A square has right angles.

   (D)   A square has parallel sides.

2. **How is a cone similar to a pyramid?**

   (F)   They both look like circles.

   (G)   They both look like squares.

   (H)   They both look like rectangles.

   (J)   They both look like triangles.

3. **Which of these shapes does not have any sides or angles?**

   (A)

   (B)

   (C)

   (D)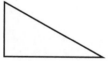

4. **Which of these shapes has one less angle than a square?**

   (F)

   (G)

   (H)

   (J)

5. **Which of these shapes has one more side than a square?**

   (A)

   (B)

   (C)

   (D)

Mathematics

3.B

Using a Coordinate Grid

Geometry

DIRECTIONS: Use the grid to answer each question.

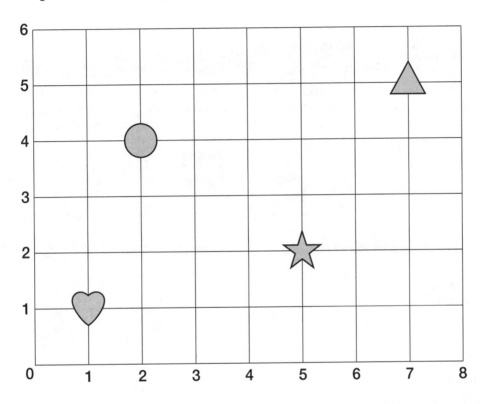

 Clue   Always start at 0 when naming locations on a grid. Move right first and then move up to find each shape.

1. **From 0, which shape is found 5 to the right and 2 up?**

   (A) heart

   (B) circle

   (C) star

   (D) triangle

2. **From 0, which shape is found 2 to the right and 4 up?**

   (F) heart

   (G) circle

   (H) star

   (J) triangle

3. **From the star, how do you get to the triangle?**

   (A) go right 2 lines, up 3 lines

   (B) go right 1 line, up 1 line

   (C) go right 3 lines, up 3 lines

   (D) go right 2 lines, up 1 line

4. **From the heart, how do you get to the circle?**

   (F) go right 2 lines, up 2 lines

   (G) go right 2 lines, up 3 lines

   (H) go right 1 line, up 3 lines

   (J) go right 1 line, up 1 line

Transformations

Geometry

DIRECTIONS: Study the examples. Then, look at each pair of shapes. Decide if the shapes show a flip, turn, or slide.

Examples:

If you **flip** a shape, it looks like its mirror image.

If you **turn** a shape, it looks like the same shape, just turned one way or the other.

If you **slide** a shape, its looks like the same shape in a different location.

1.

(A) flip
(B) turn
(C) slide
(D) none of the above

2.

(F) flip
(G) turn
(H) slide
(J) none of the above

3.

(A) flip
(B) turn
(C) slide
(D) none of the above

4.

(F) flip
(G) turn
(H) slide
(J) none of the above

5.

(A) flip
(B) turn
(C) slide
(D) none of the above

6.

(F) flip
(G) turn
(H) slide
(J) none of the above

STOP

Mathematics

3.C

Symmetry

Geometry

DIRECTIONS: Choose the best answer.

Example:

A **line of symmetry** is a line that divides a picture or shape into two equal halves. If you fold the shape along the line, both sides will match.

Both sides will match when this is folded along the dotted line.

These sides will not match when this is folded along the dotted line.

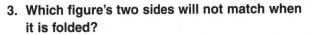

---

1. **What shape would you have if you cut the egg exactly in half?**

Ⓐ   Ⓑ   Ⓒ   Ⓓ

2. **Which shape would you have if you cut the book exactly in half?**

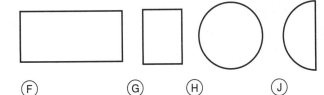

Ⓕ   Ⓖ   Ⓗ   Ⓙ

3. **Which figure's two sides will not match when it is folded?**

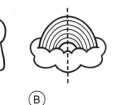

Ⓐ   Ⓑ   Ⓒ   Ⓓ

4. **If you fold one of these figures in half, two of the sides will match exactly. Which figure is it?**

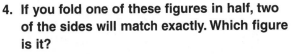

Ⓕ   Ⓖ   Ⓗ   Ⓙ

STOP

3.D

Recognizing Different Perspectives
Geometry

Below are two-dimensional views of the three-dimensional shape on the left.

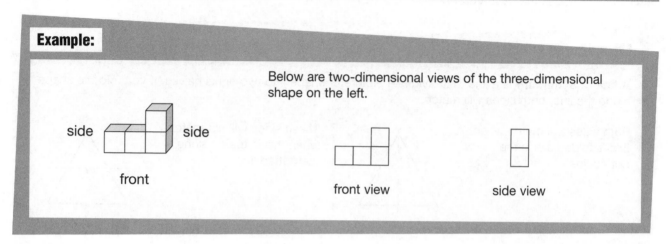

side   side

front

front view   side view

DIRECTIONS: Look at the three-dimensional shape. Then, picture the shape from the side or the front. Choose the best answer.

1. **Which of these views shows this set of cubes from the side?**

side
front

(A)

(C) ▯ (vertical three)

(B) ☐

(D) none of the above

2. **Which of these views shows this set of cubes from the front?**

side
front

(F)

(H)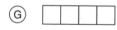

(G)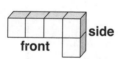

(J) none of the above

DIRECTIONS: Use the following objects to help you answer questions 3–5.

3. **Which one of these objects does not roll well?**

(A) cylinder
(B) cube
(C) cone
(D) sphere

4. **Which one of these does not have any flat surfaces?**

(F) cylinder
(G) cone
(H) sphere
(J) cube

5. **Which one of these does not have any view that would be a circle?**

(A) cone
(B) sphere
(C) cylinder
(D) cube

Name _____   Date _____

Mathematics

Using Measurement

Measurement

DIRECTIONS: Choose the best answer.

1. **Which one of these objects might weigh 10 pounds?**

   (A)   (B)   (C)   (D)

2. **Which one of these objects is about an inch long in real life?**

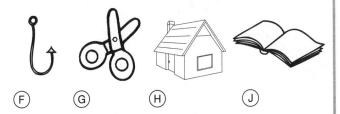

   (F)   (G)   (H)   (J)

3. **Which one of these objects can hold about 1 cup of liquid?**

   (A)   (B)   (C)   (D)

4. **Which one of these objects weighs about 12 ounces?**

   (F)   (G)   (H)   (J)

5. **Which of these units would be the best to measure how wide a room is?**
   (A) inches
   (B) feet
   (C) pounds
   (D) miles

6. **Which of these units would be the best to weigh a person?**
   (F) inches
   (G) feet
   (H) pounds
   (J) miles

7. **Which of these units would be the best to measure the length of a book?**
   (A) inches
   (B) feet
   (C) pounds
   (D) miles

8. **Which of these units would be the best to measure the distance between two cities?**
   (F) inches
   (G) feet
   (H) pounds
   (J) miles

STOP

Describing Time

Measurement

DIRECTIONS: Choose the best answer.

1. **What time does the clock show?**

   (A)   9:15

   (B)   10:30

   (C)   11:45

   (D)   11:15

2. **Look at the clock face. Find the digital clock that shows the same time.**

   (F)   11:30

   (G)    10:30

   (H)    1:00

   (J)   6:53

3. **Look at each clock. The first one shows what time the children went to the park. The second one shows what time they left the park. How long were they at the park?**

   (A)   2 hours

   (B)   20 minutes

   (C)   5 hours

   (D)   8 hours

4. **Look at the digital clock. Find the clock face that shows the same time.**

5:15

   (F)

   (G)

   (H)

   (J)

5. **The time the clock shows is thirty minutes after what time?**

   (A)   6:00

   (B)   3:00

   (C)   8:00

   (D)   7:00

STOP

Name _____   Date _____

Using Objects to Measure

Measurement

DIRECTIONS: Choose the best answer.

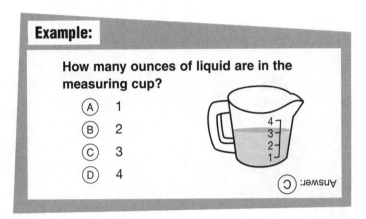

Example:

How many ounces of liquid are in the measuring cup?

(A) 1

(B) 2

(C) 3

(D) 4

Answer: (C)

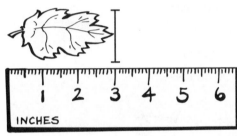

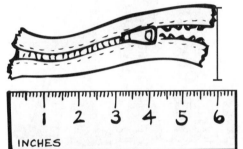

1. Look at the rulers and the items pictured. What is the difference in length between the leaf and the zipper?

(A) 3 inches

(B) 5 inches

(C) 13 inches

(D) 15 inches

2. How long are the leaf and the zipper if you put them together?

(F) 5 inches

(G) 7 inches

(H) 9 inches

(J) 11 inches

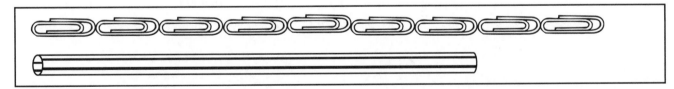

3. How many paper clips long is the drinking straw?

(A) 10 paper clips

(B) 4 paper clips

(C) 20 paper clips

(D) 7 paper clips

4. If each paper clip is about an inch long, how long is the drinking straw?

(F) 4 inches

(G) 7 inches

(H) 10 inches

(J) 20 inches

GO ⇒

5. Look at the measuring tape. Look at the people. How tall is the shortest person?

- Ⓐ 1 $\frac{1}{2}$ feet
- Ⓑ 3 feet
- Ⓒ 4 feet
- Ⓓ 6 feet

6. Which of the people above might weigh 180 pounds?

- Ⓕ the baby
- Ⓖ the young boy
- Ⓗ the older boy
- Ⓙ the man

7. About how long is this pencil in real life?

- Ⓐ 1 inch
- Ⓑ 1 foot
- Ⓒ 7 inches
- Ⓓ 2 feet

8. About how many ounces will this can hold in real life?

- Ⓕ 12 ounces
- Ⓖ 30 ounces
- Ⓗ 50 ounces
- Ⓙ 100 ounces

9. About how much does this bag of flour weigh in real life?

- Ⓐ 10 ounces
- Ⓑ 5 pounds
- Ⓒ 30 pounds
- Ⓓ 100 pounds

STOP

Name _____   Date _____

Mathematics

For pages 76–86

Mini-Test 2

Geometry; Measurement

DIRECTIONS: Choose the best answer.

1. Which picture looks like a sphere?

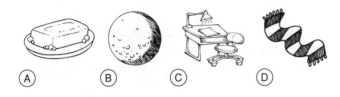

Ⓐ   Ⓑ   Ⓒ   Ⓓ

2. How many of these shapes have four or more sides?

Ⓕ 2
Ⓖ 3
Ⓗ 4
Ⓙ 5

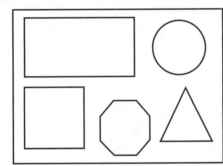

3. How many more cones are there than cubes?

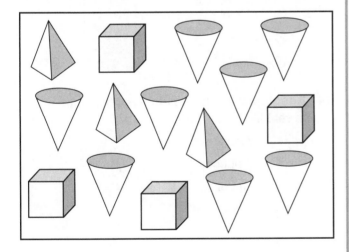

Ⓐ 2
Ⓑ 3
Ⓒ 4
Ⓓ 5

4. What shapes would you have if you cut this shape in half?

Ⓕ two squares
Ⓖ two circles
Ⓗ two rectangles
Ⓙ two triangles

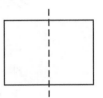

DIRECTIONS: Use the grid below to answer questions 5 and 6.

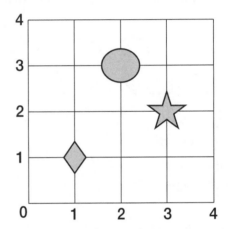

5. From 0, which shape is found 3 to the right and 2 up?

Ⓐ diamond
Ⓑ circle
Ⓒ star
Ⓓ none of the above

6. From the diamond, how do you get to the circle?

Ⓕ go right 2 lines, up 2 lines
Ⓖ go right 1 line, up 2 lines
Ⓗ go right 2 lines, up 1 line
Ⓙ go right 3 lines, up 2 lines

GO

Name _____ Date _____

DIRECTIONS: Choose the best answer.

7. **What kind of change to the shape on the left is shown here?**

    Ⓐ flip

    Ⓑ slide

    Ⓒ turn

    Ⓓ none of the above

8. **Which one of these has a side view of a square?**

    Ⓕ cone

    Ⓖ cylinder

    Ⓗ sphere

    Ⓙ cube

9. **What time does the clock show?**

    Ⓐ 9:45

    Ⓑ 10:15

    Ⓒ 10:45

    Ⓓ 11:00

10. **Look at the above clock. How long will it take for the minute hand to reach the 12?**

    Ⓕ 25 minutes

    Ⓖ 30 minutes

    Ⓗ 45 minutes

    Ⓙ 50 minutes

11. **Katarina is making a cake. Which of these units would be the best to measure how much flour she needs?**

    Ⓐ feet

    Ⓑ cups

    Ⓒ pounds

    Ⓓ inches

12. **Look at the ruler. About how long is the pair of scissors in inches?**

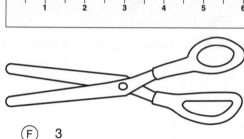

    Ⓕ 3

    Ⓖ 4

    Ⓗ 5

    Ⓙ 6

13. **About how tall is this can in real life?**

    Ⓐ 1 inch

    Ⓑ 1 foot

    Ⓒ 5 feet

    Ⓓ 5 inches

14. **About how much does this apple weigh in real life?**

    Ⓕ 7 ounces

    Ⓖ 7 pounds

    Ⓗ 20 ounces

    Ⓙ 20 pounds

STOP

Name _____   Date _____

Mathematics

5.A

Gathering and Graphing Data

Data Analysis and Probability

DIRECTIONS: Tia was helping out in her dad's shoe store. She thinks that the store sells more of some sizes than others. Tia kept track of how many shoes were sold in each size for three days. Her results are shown in the table below. Use the table to help you complete the pictograph. Draw one shoe for each pair of shoes that were sold. The results for the size 5 shoes have already been added to the graph.

 A **pictograph** uses a symbol or picture to stand for a number on a graph.
The key will tell you the number that each picture stands for.

Shoe Size	Total Pairs Sold	Shoe Size	Total Pairs Sold
5	3	8	6
6	10	9	2
7	8		

Shoe Size	Total Pairs Sold
5	🥾 🥾 🥾
6	
7	
8	
9	

 = 1 pair of shoes sold

Mathematics

| 5.A |

Representing Data

Data Analysis and Probability

DIRECTIONS: The second-grade students in Mrs. Paul's and Miss Fanta's classes voted on where they would go on a field trip. Their votes are shown in the pictograph below. Use the pictograph to answer the questions.

Votes for Class Trip

Place	Votes
Zoo	🚹🚹🚹
Museum	🚹🚹
Theater	🚹
Nature Center	🚹🚹

KEY

🚹 = 6 students

= 3 students

1. How many students voted to go to the zoo?

   _____

2. How many students voted to go to the museum?

   _____

3. How many students voted to go to the theater?

   _____

4. How many students voted to go to the nature center?

5. Which place received the most votes?

   _____

6. Which place received the least votes?

   _____

7. What is the total number of students who voted?

   _____

STOP

Mathematics

| 5.B |

Analyzing Data

Data Analysis and Probability

DIRECTIONS: Mrs. McNeil's class made a bar graph showing the hair color of the students in her class. Use the bar graph below to answer the questions.

Hair Color	Boys	Girls
Blonde		
Light Brown		
Dark Brown		
Red		
Black		

1 2 3 4 5 6 7   1 2 3 4 5 6 7

1. **How many more girls have dark brown hair than boys?**
   - (A) 2
   - (B) 4
   - (C) 6
   - (D) 8

2. **How many boys and girls have light brown hair?**
   - (F) 11
   - (G) 9
   - (H) 12
   - (J) 8

3. **How many students are in the class?**
   - (A) 29
   - (B) 15
   - (C) 25
   - (D) 31

4. **How many more girls are in the class than boys?**
   - (F) 1
   - (G) 2
   - (H) 3
   - (J) 4

5. **Which color of hair does only 1 student have?**
   - (A) blonde
   - (B) red
   - (C) light brown
   - (D) black

6. **How many more boys have dark brown hair than blonde hair?**
   - (F) 2
   - (G) 0
   - (H) 3
   - (J) 5

STOP

Name _____   Date _____

Mathematics

| 5.C |

Describing Likelihood
of Events
Data Analysis and Probability

DIRECTIONS: The students in Ms. Johnson's class are bored with their lunches. They decide to hold a surprise lunch day. They put their sandwiches in one pile and their snacks in another. Each student will be blindfolded. They will choose one sandwich and one snack from each table. Using the information below, answer the questions.

Sandwich Type	Number
Tuna	3
Jelly	2
Turkey	5
Cheese	4
Chicken salad	1

Snack Type	Number
Cookie	6
Carrot sticks	1
Chips	3
Banana	4
Apple	2

1. **Kyle is the first student to choose a sandwich. Which type of sandwich is he most likely to pull out?**

   (A) tuna sandwich

   (B) turkey sandwich

   (C) cheese sandwich

   (D) jelly sandwich

2. **Which type of sandwich is he least likely to pull out?**

   (F) cheese sandwich

   (G) jelly sandwich

   (H) tuna sandwich

   (J) chicken salad sandwich

3. **Jenna is the first student to choose a snack. Which type of snack is she most likely to pull out?**

   (A) cookie

   (B) chips

   (C) banana

   (D) apple

4. **Which type of snack is she least likely to pull out?**

   (F) apple

   (G) chips

   (H) carrot sticks

   (J) banana

STOP

Name _____ Date _____

Mathematics

Solving Problems

Process

DIRECTIONS: Choose the best answer.

 Break each problem into parts to help you understand it.

1. There are 24 students in a class. They form teams of 6 students each. Which number sentence shows how many teams they formed?

   (A) 24 − 6
   (B) 24 ÷ 6
   (C) 4 + 6
   (D) 24 × 6

2. A rancher has 16 calves. He has 4 pens. He puts the same number of calves in each pen. Which answer shows how many calves he puts in each pen?

   (F) 🐄 🐄

   (G) 🐄 🐄 🐄 🐄 🐄 🐄

   (H) 🐄 🐄 🐄 🐄 🐄 🐄
        🐄 🐄

   (J) 🐄 🐄 🐄 🐄

3. There are 27 students in a class. Each student brings in 5 insects for a science project. How can you find the number of insects they brought in altogether?

   (A) add
   (B) subtract
   (C) multiply
   (D) divide

4. Jacob has $3.00 to buy lunch. He buys a sandwich that costs $1.50 and an orange. You want to find out how much money he has left. What other piece of information do you need?

   (F) how much the orange costs
   (G) what time Jacob ate lunch
   (H) how much the milk cost
   (J) where Jacob ate lunch

5. The trip from Homeville to Lincoln usually takes 25 minutes by car. While making the trip, the driver spent another 12 minutes getting gas and 5 minutes waiting in traffic. How long did
it take the driver to make the trip?

   (A) 32 minutes
   (B) 37 minutes
   (C) 48 minutes
   (D) 42 minutes

6. The price of milk was 75 cents. It has increased by 8 cents. What would you do to find out the new price of milk?

   (F) multiply
   (G) divide
   (H) add
   (J) subtract

STOP

Mathematics
6.B

Showing Solutions

Process

DIRECTIONS: Solve these problems in the space provided. Use words, pictures, or numbers to write directions or show steps for solving the problem.

1. There are 5 lily pads in the pond. There are 2 frogs on each lily pad. How many frogs are there altogether?

   (A)   10 frogs

   (B)   13 frogs

   (C)   8 frogs

   (D)   16 frogs

2. At the county fair, there are 2 dunking booths, 8 rides, 2 shows, 5 games, and 1 hall of mirrors. How many attractions are at the county fair altogether?

   (F)   20 attractions

   (G)   19 attractions

   (H)   16 attractions

   (J)   18 attractions

3. Taina had a rectangle made out of paper. She drew a line down the middle of the rectangle from top to bottom. Then, she drew a line through the middle of the rectangle from left to right. She then had 4 shapes drawn. What 4 shapes had she made?

   (A)   4 squares

   (B)   4 circles

   (C)   4 rectangles

   (D)   4 triangles

4. Julie bought a model robot-building kit and a model rocket-building kit for $63. She started with $80. How much money did she have left?

   (F) $27

   (G) $22

   (H) $7

   (J) $17

STOP

Mathematics

6.C

Using Mathematical Language
Process

DIRECTIONS: Choose the best answer.

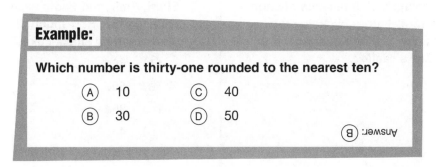

Example:

Which number is thirty-one rounded to the nearest ten?

Ⓐ 10   Ⓒ 40

Ⓑ 30   Ⓓ 50

Answer: Ⓑ

1. Which pattern shows counting by threes?

Ⓐ 3, 5, 8

Ⓑ 2, 4, 8

Ⓒ 9, 10, 11

Ⓓ 6, 9, 12

2. Which numeral shows the difference between 5 and 12?

Ⓕ 7

Ⓖ 9

Ⓗ 6

Ⓙ 5

3. The table with picture books for children was a mess. Janna sorted the books into stacks. When she was done, she had 12 stacks with 5 books in each stack. What operation will you need to use to figure out how many books there were at the sale?

Ⓐ addition

Ⓑ subtraction

Ⓒ multiplication

Ⓓ division

4. Tom has 10 balls and 3 bats. He gives Kelsey 4 balls. Then, he gives Troy 1 bat. Which operation will you need to figure out how many balls and bats Tom has left?

Ⓕ $10 + 3 - 4 - 1$

Ⓖ $10 - 3 + 4 + 1$

Ⓗ $10 - 3 + 1 - 10$

Ⓙ $10 - 4 - 3 + 1$

5. Which fraction is the same as three-quarters?

Ⓐ $\frac{1}{4}$

Ⓑ $\frac{1}{2}$

Ⓒ $\frac{3}{4}$

Ⓓ $\frac{1}{3}$

6. Which number is fifty-six plus twelve?

Ⓕ 66

Ⓖ 68

Ⓗ 58

Ⓙ 60

STOP

Name _____ Date _____

Connecting Math
to Other Areas

Process

DIRECTIONS: Choose the best answer.

1. Danny's sand castle took 9 buckets of sand to build. Gail's took 3 more buckets than Danny's. How many buckets of sand did it take to make Gail's castle?

   Ⓐ 8
   Ⓑ 12
   Ⓒ 14
   Ⓓ 3

2. Meg built a castle with 8 buckets of sand. Yolanda used the same amount. How many buckets were used altogether for the 2 castles?

   Ⓕ 20
   Ⓖ 8
   Ⓗ 16
   Ⓙ 14

3. All the children then built a huge sand castle with 13 rooms. A wave washed away 5 of the rooms. How many rooms were left?

   Ⓐ 2
   Ⓑ 4
   Ⓒ 6
   Ⓓ 8

4. Meg and Danny went to gather seashells. They had four buckets. They found 20 shells and put an equal number in each bucket. How many shells did they put in each bucket?

   Ⓕ 3
   Ⓖ 4
   Ⓗ 5
   Ⓙ 6

5. Sheri, Amir, and Paolo each bought a snack cake for 15¢. How much did they spend altogether for snack cakes?

   Ⓐ 65¢
   Ⓑ 50¢
   Ⓒ 35¢
   Ⓓ 45¢

6. Four families each gave $20 to charity. How much money did they give altogether?

   Ⓕ $24
   Ⓖ $60
   Ⓗ $84
   Ⓙ $80

7. A bus has 42 seats. Half the seats are by the window. How many seats in the bus are by the window?

   Ⓐ 21
   Ⓑ 20
   Ⓒ 12
   Ⓓ 6

8. Mr. Stricker's class lines up in 6 equal lines with 4 students in each line. How many students are in his class?

   Ⓕ 20
   Ⓖ 22
   Ⓗ 24
   Ⓙ 26

STOP

6.E
Using Representations to Solve Problems
Process

DIRECTIONS: Read each question. Then, choose the correct answer.

1. Which of these shapes can be combined to make a square?

 (A)

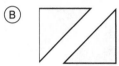 (B)

 (C)

(D)

2. Look at the pattern. Which shape below should come next in the pattern?

 ?

(F)

(G)

(H)

(J)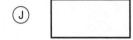

3. The computer screen shows some of the top scores earned on a computer game. Ricky earned the top score at level 10. Which score was most likely his?

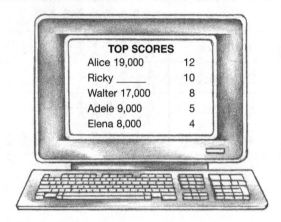

TOP SCORES	
Alice 19,000	12
Ricky _____	10
Walter 17,000	8
Adele 9,000	5
Elena 8,000	4

(A) 17,000   (C) 20,000

(B) 18,000   (D) 21,000

DIRECTIONS: The second-grade students at Zinser Elementary were asked to do reports on one of the following five birds: hummingbird, hawk, owl, blue jay, or pelican. Use the graph below to answer the question.

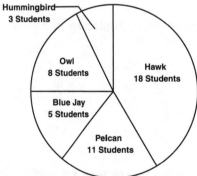

Hummingbird 3 Students

Owl 8 Students

Hawk 18 Students

Blue Jay 5 Students

Pelican 11 Students

4. Which was the favorite bird?

(F) owl

(G) blue jay

(H) pelican

(J) hawk

STOP

Mathematics

| 5.A–6.E |

For pages 89–97

Mini-Test 3

Data Analysis and Probability; Processes

DIRECTIONS: Use the pictograph below to answer questions 1–3.

Number of Students at Highview School

Grade Level	Number of Students
Kindergarten	𝌀𝌀𝌀𝌀𝌀𝌀𝌀𝌀𝌀
1st Grade	𝌀𝌀𝌀𝌀𝌀𝌀𝌀𝌀𝌀𝌀𝌀𝌀𝌀
2nd Grade	𝌀𝌀𝌀𝌀𝌀𝌀
3rd Grade	𝌀𝌀𝌀𝌀𝌀𝌀𝌀𝌀
4th Grade	𝌀𝌀𝌀𝌀𝌀𝌀𝌀𝌀𝌀𝌀𝌀𝌀
5th Grade	𝌀𝌀𝌀𝌀𝌀𝌀𝌀

Key: 𝌀 = 5 students

1. **Which grade level has the fewest number of students?**

    Ⓐ Kindergarten

    Ⓑ 1st grade

    Ⓒ 2nd grade

    Ⓓ 3rd grade

2. **How many Highview students are fourth graders?**

    Ⓕ 30

    Ⓖ 40

    Ⓗ 50

    Ⓙ 60

3. **Which two grades are tied to be the largest?**

    Ⓐ 1st and 5th

    Ⓑ 1st and 4th

    Ⓒ 2nd and 4th

    Ⓓ 1st and 3rd

DIRECTIONS: Use the graph below to answer questions 4–6.

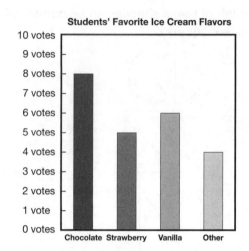

4. **How many students named vanilla as their favorite?**

    Ⓕ 2

    Ⓖ 6

    Ⓗ 8

    Ⓙ 4

5. **How many more students voted for chocolate ice cream than for strawberry?**

    Ⓐ 3

    Ⓑ 8

    Ⓒ 13

    Ⓓ 6

6. **How many students voted altogether?**

    Ⓕ 19

    Ⓖ 23

    Ⓗ 18

    Ⓙ 22

GO

DIRECTIONS: Brad put 5 red jelly beans, 4 green jelly beans, 2 yellow jelly beans, and 1 purple jelly bean in a jar. His sister closed her eyes and pulled out one at a time.

7. **Which color will his sister most likely pull out?**

   (A) green

   (B) red

   (C) yellow

   (D) purple

8. **Which color will his sister least likely pull out?**

   (F) green

   (G) red

   (H) yellow

   (J) purple

DIRECTIONS: Choose the best answer.

9. **What shape is missing from this pattern?**

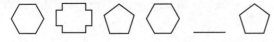

   (A)

   (B)

   (C)

   (D) none of the above

10. **What number is missing in this pattern?**

    8, 12, _____, 20, 24

    (F) 16

    (G) 4

    (H) 15

    (J) 19

11. **Ricky carried 4 boxes of tiles into the kitchen. Each box held 12 tiles. What would you do to find out how many tiles he carried into the kitchen altogether?**

    (A) add

    (B) subtract

    (C) divide

    (D) multiply

DIRECTIONS: Solve questions 12 and 13. Use words, numbers, or pictures to show your answer in the space below each problem.

12. **A waiter put 4 napkins on each table. There were 3 tables total. The waiter placed a total of _____ napkins on the tables.**

    (F) 7

    (G) 8

    (H) 12

    (J) 16

13. **There are 24 students in Tony's class. Sixteen of the students are girls. How many are boys?**

    (A) 8

    (B) 9

    (C) 10

    (D) 12

STOP

How Am I Doing?

Mini-Test 1	14–16 answers correct	**Great Job!** Move on to the section test on page 101.
Pages 74–75 **Number Correct**	9–13 answers correct	**You're almost there!** But you still need a little practice. Review practice pages 57–73 before moving on to the section test on page 101.
	0–8 answers correct	**Oops!** Time to review what you have learned and try again. Review the practice section on pages 57–73. Then, retake the test on pages 74–75. Now, move on to the section test on page 101.

Mini-Test 2	11–14 answers correct	**Awesome!** Move on to the section test on page 101.
Pages 87–88 **Number Correct**	6–10 answers correct	**You're almost there!** But you still need a little practice. Review practice pages 76–86 before moving on to the section test on page 101.
	0–5 answers correct	**Oops!** Time to review what you have learned and try again. Review the practice section on pages 76–86. Then, retake the test on pages 87–88. Now, move on to the section test on page 101.

Mini-Test 3	11–13 answers correct	**Great Job!** Move on to the section test on page 101.
Pages 98–99 **Number Correct**	6–10 answers correct	**You're almost there!** But you still need a little practice. Review practice pages 89–97 before moving on to the section test on page 101.
	0–5 answers correct	**Oops!** Time to review what you have learned and try again. Review the practice section on pages 89–97. Then, retake the test on pages 98–99. Now, move on to the section test on page 101.

Name _____   Date _____

Final Mathematics Test
for pages 57–99

DIRECTIONS: Choose the best answer.

1. Look at the base ten blocks. What is the number shown here?

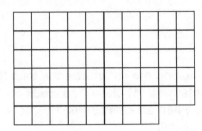

  Ⓐ 55
  Ⓑ 58
  Ⓒ 68
  Ⓓ 72

2. Which number is between twenty-three and thirty-four?

  Ⓕ 19
  Ⓖ 40
  Ⓗ 30
  Ⓙ 20

3. Look at the following set of numbers. What is the place value of the 3s?

31   437   5,239

  Ⓐ ones
  Ⓑ tens
  Ⓒ hundreds
  Ⓓ thousands

4. Look at the chart below. What number is shown?

100s	10s	1s
●● ●● ●● ●●	●● ●	●● ●● ●

  Ⓕ 745
  Ⓖ 935
  Ⓗ 837
  Ⓙ 835

5. Which fraction shows how much of the bar is shaded?

  Ⓐ $\frac{3}{5}$
  Ⓑ $\frac{1}{4}$
  Ⓒ $\frac{1}{2}$
  Ⓓ $\frac{2}{5}$

6. Which number should go in the boxes to make both number sentences true?

  $8 + \square = 22$

  $22 - \square = 8$

  Ⓕ 12
  Ⓖ 14
  Ⓗ 16
  Ⓙ 18

GO ➡

Name _____   Date _____

7. Look at the pattern. Which shape comes next?

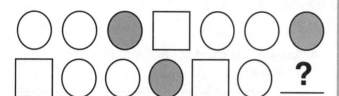

(A) gray circle

(B) square

(C) circle

(D) gray triangle

8. If **+ 7 = 23, what is** ☆ **?**

(F) 8

(G) 16

(H) 14

(J) 7

9. If 47 − ☐ = 29, what is ☐?

(A) 22

(B) 17

(C) 42

(D) 18

10. What is the name of this figure?

(F) sphere

(G) cone

(H) cube

(J) cylinder

11. What shape would you have if you folded this kite in half?

(A) circle

(B) square

(C) triangle

(D) rectangle

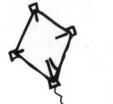

12. How many fish long is this chain?

(F) 6 fish

(G) 2 fish

(H) 4 fish

(J) 5 fish

13. The clock on the left shows the time the students have art class. The clock on the right shows when art class ends. How long does art class last?

(A) 1 hour

(B) 2 hours

(C) 45 minutes

(D) 30 minutes

14. About how much water can this glass hold in real life?

(F) 2 ounces

(G) 10 ounces

(H) 50 ounces

(J) 100 ounces

15. About how tall is the average second grader?

(A) 1 foot

(B) 4 feet

(C) 6 feet

(D) 10 feet

GO

DIRECTIONS: Use this pictograph to answer questions 16–18.

Birthdays	
January	🧍 🧍 🧍
February	🧍 🧍
March	🧍 ⌐
April	🧍 🧍 🧍 🧍
May	🧍 🧍 ⌐
June	⌐

KEY: 🧍 = 2 students

⌐ = 1 student

16. **How many students have birthdays in March and April?**

   (F) 11
   (G) 5
   (H) 12
   (J) 6

17. **How many more students have birthdays in January than February?**

   (A) 5
   (B) 2
   (C) 4
   (D) 3

18. **How many total students have birthdays in January through June?**

   (F) 24
   (G) 27
   (H) 20
   (J) 26

DIRECTIONS: Read each story problem. Then, choose the best answer.

19. **Marcel has a bag of marbles. There are 6 blue, 3 red, 2 orange, and 1 green. If he pulls out a marble without looking, which color is he least likely to grab?**

   (A) red
   (B) blue
   (C) green
   (D) orange

20. **There are 28 students in a class. If they break up into 4 equal teams, which number sentence shows how many students will be on each team?**

   (F) $28 - 4 = 24$
   (G) $28 \div 4 = 7$
   (H) $28 + 4 = 32$
   (J) $28 \times 4 = 112$

21. **Becky has 18 jelly beans on her desk. Michael has 26 jelly beans on his desk. How many more jelly beans does Michael have than Becky?**

   (A) 6
   (B) 16
   (C) 18
   (D) 8

22. **Ricco's photo album has 9 pictures on each page. There are 20 full pages in the album. What would you do to find out how many pictures Ricco has in his album altogether?**

   (F) add
   (G) subtract
   (H) multiply
   (J) divide

STOP

Final Mathematics Test
Answer Sheet

1 (A) (B) (C) (D)
2 (F) (G) (H) (J)
3 (A) (B) (C) (D)
4 (F) (G) (H) (J)
5 (A) (B) (C) (D)
6 (F) (G) (H) (J)
7 (A) (B) (C) (D)
8 (F) (G) (H) (J)
9 (A) (B) (C) (D)
10 (F) (G) (H) (J)

11 (A) (B) (C) (D)
12 (F) (G) (H) (J)
13 (A) (B) (C) (D)
14 (F) (G) (H) (J)
15 (A) (B) (C) (D)
16 (F) (G) (H) (J)
17 (A) (B) (C) (D)
18 (F) (G) (H) (J)
19 (A) (B) (C) (D)
20 (F) (G) (H) (J)

21 (A) (B) (C) (D)
22 (F) (G) (H) (J)

Answer Key

Pages 7–8
1. D
2. H
3. B
4. H
5. C
6. H
7. D
8. H

Pages 9–10
1. C
2. G
3. C
4. J
5. A
6. H
7. B
8. F

Pages 11–12
1. C
2. G
3. C
4. J
5. A
6. G
7. C
8. H
9. C
10. G
11. A
12. G
13. D
14. H

Pages 13–14
1. B
2. G
3. D
4. F
5. D
6. G
7. C
8. F

Page 15
1. B
2. H
3. B
4. J
5. D
6. F

Pages 16–17
1. A
2. H
3. C
4. F
5. B
6. F
7. A
8. G
9. C
10. J

Page 18
1. A
2. H
3. D
4. G
5. B
6. F

Page 19
1. A
2. H
3. B
4. J
5. C

Page 20
1. B
2. H
3. A
4. H

Page 21
1. A
2. H
3. D
4. F

Pages 22–23
Mini-Test 1
1. A
2. H
3. D
4. H
5. A
6. F
7. D
8. H
9. B
10. G
11. B
12. G
13. C

Pages 24–25
1. A
2. J
3. C
4. G
5. C
6. G
7. A
8. J
9. C
10. G
11. D

Page 26
1. A
2. G
3. C
4. H
5. A
6. F

Page 27
1. D
2. G
3. C
4. F
5. D
6. G

Page 28
1. C
2. F
3. D
4. G
5. D
6. H

Page 29
1. A
2. G

Page 30
1. A
2. H
3. D
4. G
5. C
6. J

Page 31
1. C
2. J
3. A
4. G
5. A
6. H

Page 32
1. C
2. G
3. C

Page 33
Topic sentence: Many insects find a <u>warm</u> place to spend the <u>winter</u>. Supporting details: Ants dig deep in the ground. Beetles stack up under rocks or dead leaves. Female grasshoppers die before winter. Bees gather in a ball in the hive.

Pages 34–35
1. C
2. J
3. B
4. J
5. A
6. G
7. A
8. G
9. A
10. F
11. C
12. G

Page 36
1. D
2. H
3. A
4. J
5. C
6. F

Page 37
1. C
2. G
3. C
4. F
5. C
6. G

Page 38
1. D
2. G
3. C
4. F
5. B
6. H

Pages 39–40
Mini-Test 2
1. A
2. J
3. D
4. H
5. A
6. G
7. C
8. J
9. D
10. G
11. A
12. F
13. B
14. H

Page 41
1. C
2. Students should write two questions about therapy dogs.
3. G
4. Students should write two questions about jellyfish.

Page 42
1. B
2. J
3. B
4. F
5. C
6. G

Page 43
1. D
2. J
3. A
4. G
5. B
6. J

Page 44
Mini-Test 3
1. A
2. H
3. B
4. G
5. D
6. F
7. D

Page 45
1. D
2. H
3. B
4. H

Page 46
Students should draw a picture about something they did or did not like about the book. Students should then write a couple of sentences that explain their drawing.

Page 47
1. Students should write the name of their favorite book.
2. Students should check all of the boxes that apply to their book.
3. Students should describe what their book was about.

4. Students should explain why they would recommend this book to others.

Page 48
Mini-Test 4
1. D
2. G
3. B
4. H

Pages 51–53
Final English
Language Arts Test
1. C
2. G
3. D
4. H
5. C
6. F
7. D
8. F
9. C
10. J
11. B
12. J
13. D
14. H
15. A
16. H
17. A
18. G
19. C
20. H
21. D
22. G
23. A
24. H
25. B
26. J
27. A

Pages 57–58
1. D
2. F
3. A
4. H
5. A
6. J
7. A
8. H
9. C
10. H
11. C
12. G

Page 59
1. A
2. G
3. C
4. G
5. B
6. F
7. C
8. J

Page 60
1. D
2. J
3. B
4. F
5. $\frac{4}{5}$
6. $\frac{1}{2}$
7. $\frac{4}{6}$
8. $\frac{3}{4}$
9. $\frac{1}{4}$
10. $\frac{2}{3}$

Page 61
1. D
2. G
3. B
4. F
5. D

Page 62
1. A
2. H
3. B
4. G
5. C
6. G

Page 63
1. 12
2. 5
3. 14
4. 10
5. 9
6. 8

Page 64
1. 4
2. 5
3. 2
4. 2
5. 2
6. 3

Page 65
1. B
2. H
3. A
4. J
5. C
6. F
7. C
8. J
9. C
10. F
11. A
12. J

Page 66
1. B
2. F
3. A
4. G
5. D
6. G
7. B
8. J
9. D
10. H
11. B
12. J

Page 67
1. C
2. F
3. C
4. G
5. D
6. J
7. C
8. J

Page 68
1. C
2. G
3. B
4. J
5. C
6. F
7. C
8. G
9. A

Page 69
1. D
2. H
3. B
4. J
5. B
6. J
7. B

Page 70
1. A
2. H
3. B
4. H
5. A
6. G
7. C

Page 71
1. C
2. G
3. A
4. J
5. C
6. G
7. D

Page 72
1. A
2. H
3. D
4. F
5. C
6. G

Page 73
1. A
2. J
3. B
4. H
5. D
6. F

Pages 74–75
Mini-Test 1
1. B
2. H
3. A
4. J
5. C

6. F
7. D
8. G
9. B
10. F
11. B
12. H
13. C
14. G
15. A
16. J

Pages 76–77
1. C
2. G
3. C
4. H
5. D
6. H
7. D
8. H
9. B
10. F
11. D
12. H
13. D
14. F

Page 78
1. A
2. J
3. A
4. H
5. B

Page 79
1. C
2. G
3. A
4. H

Page 80
1. B
2. H
3. A
4. J
5. A
6. G

Page 81
1. B
2. G
3. D
4. G

Page 82
1. C
2. F
3. B
4. H
5. D

Page 83
1. D
2. F
3. B
4. J
5. B
6. H
7. A
8. J

Page 84
1. D
2. G
3. A
4. H
5. C

Pages 85–86
1. A
2. H
3. D
4. G
5. A
6. J
7. C
8. F
9. B

Pages 87–88
Mini-Test 2
1. B
2. G
3. C
4. H
5. C
6. G
7. A
8. J
9. B
10. H
11. B
12. J
13. D
14. F

Shoe Size	Total Pairs Sold
5	(3 shoes)
6	(10 shoes)
7	(8 shoes)
8	(6 shoes)
9	(2 shoes)

Page 90
1. 21 students
2. 12 students
3. 9 students
4. 15 students
5. the zoo
6. the theater
7. 57 votes

Page 91
1. A
2. H
3. A
4. F
5. B
6. H

Page 92
1. B
2. J
3. A
4. H

Page 93
1. B
2. J
3. C
4. F
5. D
6. H

Page 94
1. A
2. J
3. C
4. J

Page 95
1. D
2. F
3. C
4. F
5. C
6. G

Page 96
1. B
2. H
3. D
4. H
5. D
6. J
7. A
8. H

Page 97
1. B
2. G
3. B
4. J

Pages 98–99
Mini-Test 3
1. C
2. J
3. B
4. G
5. A
6. G
7. B
8. J
9. C
10. F
11. D
12. H

13. A

Pages 101–103
Final Mathematics Test
1. B
2. H
3. B
4. J
5. D
6. G
7. C
8. G
9. D
10. F
11. C
12. J
13. A
14. G
15. B
16. F
17. B
18. G
19. C
20. G
21. D
22. H

NOTES

NOTES

NOTES

NOTES